Law and the Kinetic Environment

AF706846

This book addresses the legal-geographical implications of the fact that landscapes are not static, but dynamic. Within the field of legal geography, the spatial relationship of law to landscape is usually considered to be static. Environments are often considered fixed, and consequently inert, as places that literally don't go anywhere. Typically, then, it is what happens in these places, rather than the place itself, that commands academic attention. In contrast to this static viewpoint, *Law and the Kinetic Environment* considers how many landscapes are in flux and, as a result, may be seen as dynamic. Natural phenomena, such as oozing lava, moving glaciers, or bubbling geothermal pools, challenge and test the normative conceptualizations of stability of place, property ownership, and legal regulation. Consequently, such dynamic landscapes enliven and transform law, offering new jurisprudential insights into what law is and how it operates in response to the kineticism that, this book argues is, to some degree, inherent in all landscapes. This original engagement with legal geography will appeal to those with general interests in this area, as well as specific concerns with questions of law and place, property and the environment.

Sarah Marusek is Associate Professor and Chair of the Political Science Department at the University of Hawai'i Hilo

Space, Materiality and the Normative

Series Editors: Andreas Philippopoulos-Mihalopoulos and Christian Borch

Space, Materiality and the Normative presents new ways of thinking about the connections between space and materiality from a normative perspective. At the interface of law, social theory, politics, architecture, geography and urban studies, the series is concerned with addressing the use, regulation and experience of space and materiality, broadly understood, and in particular with exploring their links and the challenges they raise for law, politics and normativity.

https://www.routledge.com/Space-Materiality-and-the-Normative/book-series/SMNORM

Law and the Kinetic Environment

Regulating Dynamic Landscapes

Sarah Marusek

Routledge
Taylor & Francis Group
LONDON AND NEW YORK

First published 2021
by Routledge
2 Park Square, Milton Park, Abingdon, Oxon OX14 4RN

and by Routledge
52 Vanderbilt Avenue, New York, NY 10017

Routledge is an imprint of the Taylor & Francis Group, an informa business

© 2021 **Sarah Marusek**

The right of **Sarah Marusek** to be identified as author[/s] of this work has been asserted by him/her/them in accordance with sections 77 and 78 of the Copyright, Designs and Patents Act 1988.

All rights reserved. No part of this book may be reprinted or reproduced or utilised in any form or by any electronic, mechanical, or other means, now known or hereafter invented, including photocopying and recording, or in any information storage or retrieval system, without permission in writing from the publishers.

Trademark notice: Product or corporate names may be trademarks or registered trademarks, and are used only for identification and explanation without intent to infringe.

British Library Cataloguing-in-Publication Data
A catalogue record for this book is available from the British Library

Library of Congress Cataloging-in-Publication Data
A catalog record has been requested for this book

ISBN: 978-1-138-23340-9 (hbk)
ISBN: 978-1-315-30937-8 (ebk)

Typeset in Times
by KnowledgeWorks Global Ltd.

Contents

List of figures vi
Preface viii

1 Fluidity of land, lava, and law 1

2 Epistemologies of jurisdiction 19

3 Legalizing the spectacle 37

4 Topologies of governance 57

5 Knowing the ropes 75

Concluding remarks: jurisprudence of the enlivened terrain 91

Bibliography 95
Index 103

Figures

1.1 Glow from Halema'uma'u Crater, Kīlauea Volcano at Hawai'i Volcanoes National Park (March 2013); image available at https://commons.wikimedia.org/wiki/File:Halemaumau_Crater,_March_2013.jpg 4
1.2 Strokkur Geyser, March 2016, image copyright: this author 5
2.1 Visitors admiring restored Herb Kane mural; available at https://www.nps.gov/havo/learn/news/20150921_pr_kane.htm 25
3.1 Spectators view another explosion cloud from the Volcano House Hotel at Kīlauea Volcano (May 24, 1924). Available at: https://volcanoes.usgs.gov/volcanoes/kilauea/geo_hist_1924_halemaumau.html 41
3.2 Kīlauea Iki Volcano erupting, Big Island of Hawaii (1955). Available at: https://commons.wikimedia.org/wiki/Category:Kīlauea_Iki#/media/File:Kilauea_Iki_erupting_1959.JPG 41
3.3 Visitors observe the summit eruption of Kīlauea from the safe vantage point at the observation deck at Jaggar Museum, one-mile away from Halema'uma'u Crater (2017). Available at: https://www.nps.gov/havo/learn/news/030817guide.htm 42
3.4 Lava-viewing areas (Civil Defense), Feb. 2018. Available at https://commons.wikimedia.org/wiki/File:Kalapana,_HI,_county_parking,_start_of_the_lava_trail_2018-Feb-3.jpg 49
4.1 USGS Hawai'i Island lava hazard map. Available at https://commons.wikimedia.org/wiki/File:USGS_Hawaii_Island_Lava_Hazard_Map.gif 60
4.2 Lava flow travel times based on actual flow rates 63
4.3 HVO earthquake map 64
4.4 Lava flow thickness map 65
4.5 Kīlauea Volcano – East Rife Zone, August 7, 2018 66
4.6 Fissure map 69

4.7 Lava covering pavement within the Hawai'i Volcanoes National Park. Photo credits: Phil Whitehouse, Creative Commons, Wikimedia.org. Accessed Feb. 18, 2020 at https://commons.wikimedia.org/wiki/Category:Chain_of_Craters_Road#/media/File:(Other)_End_of_the_road_(6480756615).jpg 73
5.1 The 1959 Kīlauea Iki volcano eruption 76
5.2a Sign on the rope displaying the temperature of the water 85
5.2b Strokkur Geyser 85
5.3 Warnings at Strokkur 86
5.4 Sign at Devastation Hiking Trail on crater's rim within the HVNP with enlarged detail 87

Preface

Oozing landscapes: Hawai'i and Iceland

In the middle of the Pacific Ocean, there is a volcanic archipelago known as Hawai'i. Formerly, the Kingdom of Hawai'i, Hawai'i became the fiftieth U.S. state in 1959 following the American overthrow of the Hawaiian monarchy in 1893 and the U.S. annexation of the islands in 1898. Hawai'i Island, also referred to as the Big Island, is the largest of the eight primary islands in terms of land size but smallest in terms of population. Hawai'i Island is unique among the island chain, as there are five shield volcanoes on Hawai'i Island, with Kīlauea Volcano as the most active. As a shield volcano, Kīlauea differs from the more explosive and pyroclastic stratovolcanoes. Generally speaking, the lava generated from shield volcanoes oozes while lava from stratovolcanoes explodes suddenly. As one of the most active volcanoes in the world, Kīlauea has most recently been continuously erupting from January 1983 to August 2018. While Western scientists have been recording Kīlauea's activity over the past two hundred years with recorded eruptions resulting in the consistent altering of landscape, Hawaiians and early Polynesians lived with Kīlauea's flows for thousands of years prior to Western contact.

I have called Hilo, Hawai'i, my home for nearly eleven years. Hilo is about twenty-five miles from Kilauea's Summit, Halema'uma'u Crater, lower vents at Pu'u 'Ō'ō, and most recently Fissure 8 in Leilani Estates. Soon after my arrival, I came across a man whose house was the last remaining house in the Royal Gardens subdivision inundated by a 1990 lava flow. Fascinated by the proximity of lava to his residential experience, I invited him to come and speak in my class and to share his narrative of living on a recent lava flow. However, rather than talking about living with lava, the man's narrative was more a narrative of home ownership gone awry involving banks, local taxation authorities, and environmental regulations that restricted him from hosting helicopter tours from his house, a converted bed and breakfast. Yet, his resulting property narrative nonetheless followed the activity of this dynamic landscape. In his own words, he "could outrun Madame

Pele" and stated that his more immediate concerns involved the threats of tsunami, earthquake, and/or hurricane and not so much the movement of lava. However, since his guest lecture to my class in the Fall of 2010, his house, the final structure in the Royal Gardens subdivision, was covered by lava in 2012 (*Hawaii News Now* 2012). While he may have outrun Pele, the Hawaiian goddess of fire and the volcano, his house could not.

Since then, the lava in the crater has risen and fallen with lava oozing from Pu'u 'Ō'ō in its flow to the ocean. In 2014, lava pushed its way towards the village of Pāhoa. Most recently, in the summer of 2018, lava erupted somewhat more vigorously in the middle of the residential subdivisions, Leilani Estates and Lanipuna Gardens. As of this writing, lava erupting from this most recent Leilani eruption has been unprecedented in the recorded history of the past two hundred years.

Fascinated by law's response as a resident of a volcanically active island, I traveled to Iceland in 2016 to research the relationship of tourism to law in volcanic environments. Iceland and Hawai'i are strikingly similar places, as both islands are spectacles of nature. Both places reveal insight into the spectacle and subsequential relationship between law and place. Both are islands that host rural populations amidst myriad active volcanoes. Both types of volcanoes in both places are shield volcanoes. In Iceland, lava tends to flow underneath glacial ice and comes to the surface/erupts in various places. In Hawaii, lava tends to flows inside the boundaries of the Hawai'i Volcanoes National Park (HVNP), but more recently, outside park boundaries in private subdivisions, such as Royal Gardens or Leilani Estates. In Iceland, many of the volcanoes, particularly Katla, erupt under glaciers away from villages, but at other times near villages. Because most of these volcanoes are within national parks and this situation seems similar to that of the HVNP, I become quite interested in the publicly accessible and unregulated Strokkur Geyser, which is not within a national park.

Because lava in Iceland seems to be more removed from such direct contact with communities as in Hawai'i, I took interest in the geothermal bubbling of water as a landscape that is similar to that of Kīlauea and Hawai'i Island in terms of culture, tourism, and fundamentally living within such a kinetic environment. Throughout Iceland, natural spas and geysers decorate the landscape. Geothermal hotspots such as Iceland's Strokkur Geyser and the Blue Lagoon may be comparable to Kīlauea's lava in terms of the dynamism of the earth that happens below the feet and results in legalized regulation. Molten lava and bubbling boiling water are spectacles of nature.

And, then there's Iceland's Þingvellir (Thingvellir) National Park where the two continental plates of Europe and North America meet. Visitors can walk between them as they move, as the movement of this spectacle is quite slow, with an average of 1 mm to 18-mm per year (Bain and Averbuck 2015, 107). Like Kīlauea, Thingvellir is a UNESCO World Heritage Site, and timing is crucial to the movement of this place as well as the geysers and

Kīlauea's lava. As the landscape moves, whether slowly as with Thingvellir, more routinely as with Strokkur Geyser, or in spurts and oozes as with Kīlauea's lava, law follows the movement. The timing of law results from the movement of law in these dynamic environments.

With Iceland as place of comparison, Kīlauea is the primary example of the kinetic environment that drives this book, as it is what I personally know and experience on a daily basis, but also for the reason that it provides keen insight into American law. I am not Hawaiian, but a ha'ole transplant from the mainland. My position as a researcher is one of respectful observer and possibly perpetual tourist as it frames my perspectives of both Iceland and Hawai'i. As a socio-legal researcher, my positionality compels me to see multiple aspects of law as a constant presence in both places. With this being said, both places are culturally unique and distinct with regard to law's function and purpose with regard to the spectacle of the dynamic landscape.

Law and the kinetic environment: regulating the dynamic landscape

In this book, I am writing about law and the moving landscape. Lava generates one such landscape. Geysers create another. Typically, landscapes are static, stable, and not in motion. Examples of this type of landscape might include the built environment or natural landscapes that remain still and are not motile. However, some landscapes move, and through this movement, are governed according to the frameworks of law, such as ownership, control, and common sense. For example, the lava at Kīlauea Volcano on Hawai'i Island was governed through the creation of the HVNP as an extension of ownership by the U.S. government in the Territory of Hawaii. The moving landscape of this volcanic environment was a threat to the order of American law and needed to be secured as a spectacle to be managed and contained under American jurisdiction. However, those lines of jurisdiction become blurred once the lava flows outside the federal boundaries of the National Park as in the 2014 Pāhoa Flow. Lava flows out of public land through private properties and complicates existing understandings of property law, nature, and law's relationship to nature; as a durable phenomenon, law seeks to govern through public's response to flowing lava through collaboration with non-legal actors, such as science, culture, and tourism. However, law's visibility in the fluid lavascape is actually an illusion of the performativity of law as law's authority may itself be based on the incomplete compliance of individual common sense.

Whether as molten rivers of lava or newly accreted land from cooled lava flows, Kīlauea dynamically (re)creates the landscape. Natural vistas as well as manmade constructions are subject to the eruptive whims of Kīlauea. In interesting and compelling ways, these changing landscapes perplex the practice and understanding Western law that is steeped in the regulation of the environment. While the perspective of law is to generally govern and guide, practical dimensions of governing a changing landscape such as Kīlauea generates new ways of seeing law's role in the environment. Furthermore, in such kinetic places, the environment itself is an evolving terrain of knowledge that challenges law's ability to govern. The dynamic landscape expands beyond the land itself to include impacted air, weather, community, science, culture, and tourism. Such landscapes are catalyzed through spectacle.

Natural landscapes that move are varied throughout the world and can range from slowly moving continental plates (as in Iceland's Thingvellir National Park), geysers (such as Iceland's Strokkur Geyser), or oozing lava flows (from Kīlauea Volcano in Hawai'i) to more sudden events that include abrupt movements of land (earthquakes), unexpected deluges of water (floods and tsunamis), and violent storms of wildfires. This book will examine the slower, less drastic, yet equally significant movements of earth in two similar parts of the world: Hawai'i Island and Iceland. In attempts to manage the predictable, yet ultimately independent movement of land, natural phenomena related to lava and geothermal bubbling obliges law to engender a localized regulatory response to jurisdictional frameworks of risk, hazard, and regulations associated with terrestrial flow. Within the contemporary societies of Hawai'i and Iceland, the dynamic landscape frames law's relationship to people and property in ongoing, continuously evolving ways. The public space constructed around these sites of spectacle characterizes law's relationship with materiality and fluidity through a variety of regulatory practices. Such practices include the designation of governmental reserve, such as the national park, the establishment of ropes and signs declaring risk and advising self-responsibility, or the cultural vantage points guiding locally specific legislation regarding public space, public safety, and/or protection of the environment.

As the temporality of change in these two island settings is more often enduring rather than sudden, law and legality impacting human access to these areas exhibits kinetic frameworks of regulation. Temporal as well as spatial understandings of natural phenomena relating to tourism, land management, and indigenous epistemologies contextualize boundaries in these places. Home to thriving local populations, Iceland and Hawai'i attract thousands of global tourists each year to visit an array of wonders within the volcanic environment. Here, the spectacle of nature is often framed through the legal discourses of visitation, risk, and property ownership.

In the field of legal geography, landscapes are often considered stable. In contrast to static frameworks about place that engender law to be stable and enduring, this book jurisprudentially challenges such tidy equilibriums. Landscape change produces legal frameworks of messiness, disarray, and unknowability that resist such stationary positioning. When landscapes are in motion, the movement of place engenders new ways to consider the legal relationship between nature, property, and environments. Such a movement presents a puzzle for property theorists and calls traditional notions of land ownership into question as law is in kinetic motion with the legally constitutive forces of culture, history, and politics. As a result, the dynamic landscape is temporal, spatial, and material regarding the movement of law in the present, as forecast in the future, and consequential regarding the past. The relationship between jurisprudence and landscape change serves as a metaphor for law in which visually evolving landscapes destabilize normative presentations of order and governance. Response to movement in the kinetic environment of the dynamic landscape is key to understanding how law works.

The legality generated by contained as well as unrestricted dynamic landscapes further challenges American legal standards pertaining to risk management, land ownership, and jurisdiction as premised upon stable, unchanging terrain. Additionally, the spatio-temporality of a landscape in motion raises important questions about notions of legal reasoning that jurisprudentially shapes property discourse and relationships with the environment. The study of dynamic landscapes further contributes to larger questions involving the epistemology of property, regulation, and ownership in public environments. Specifically, the concept of the dynamic landscape, in conjunction with the semiotics of regulation that manage public spaces within the volcanic environments of flowing lava in Hawai'i and geothermal bubbling in Iceland, characterizes the kineticism of the legal environment. Such semiotics of regulation include the jurisdictional creation of national or county parks that surround natural phenomena, the absence of formal boundaries in regions of natural phenomena, and structures that warn of spectacle-related risk (such as fences, boardwalks, and signs).

With these spectacles in mind, this book is about the life of law on an active volcano. More specifically, the book sees life on an active volcano in the middle of the ocean as legal metaphor. Here, lava is like law in that both operate in predictable, yet spontaneous ways. The volcano endures, but law is something newer. Western-based jurisprudence, focused on property ownership and control over the land, operates almost in contrast to the steady stream of either lava or steam found in these places. Law's forced hand of reaction must happen in response to the volcano's whims and never vice versa. The reactions of law become their own phenomenon. As the volcano and geyser are themselves spectacles, so too is law a spectacle in the volcanic environments of Hawai'i and Iceland.

The eruptive nature of volcanoes results in flowing lava whether above the earth's crust or beneath it in heated waters. This movement of molten rock results in a dynamic landscape, or kinetic environment, in which the landscape is on the move and ever-changing. The stability associated with law's ability to provide social foundations becomes a spectacle when nature confronts law. This confrontation leads to law as a spectacle in which eruption, unseen currents, but also prediction, share understandings of how life happens in ways that cause this legal foundation to evolve and respond to nature. The materiality of the spectacle, whether molten (or cooled) lava or eruptive geothermal hotspots (geysers), represents the materiality of law insofar as legal materiality, often unseen in everyday banalities provides the foundation for social order.

In writing this book, I would like to express my deep appreciation first and foremost to Andreas Philippopoulos-Mihalopoulos for believing in me and my continued creative potential for this project through numerous earthquakes, lava flows, promotions, and even a global pandemic. I would also like to express my gratitude to my family, Jon, Olive, Harriet, Anna, and Biff for their encouragement, laughter, and opened ears. Other wonderful people who have helped me through this project are Anne Wagner, Marilyn Brown, Anita Lam, Peregrine Schwartz-Shea, Samantha Majic, Kimala Price, Dvora Yanow, David Delaney, Mary Louise Haraguchi, Colin Perrin, Kirsten Møllegaard, and the following Research Assistants in the Department of Political Science at the University of Hawai'i Hilo: Puanani Kahai, Tyler Hoffman, Kyle Jones, and Alexandria Agdeppa. I would also like to thank Birna Guttormsdóttir and her colleagues in the Department of Integration at the Umhverfisstofnun, Environmental Agency of Iceland, in Reykjavik for their comparative insights about life and law on a volcanic island; additionally, Dr. Adalheidur Jóhannsdóttir, Professor of Law in the Faculty of Law at the University of Iceland in Reykjavik, for her candor in discussing tourism and law in Iceland.

I have presented aspects of this project in a variety of venues, including the Western Political Science Association (2015, 2019), Law and Society Association (2015, 2016,), Hawai'i Sociological Association (2016), American Political Science Association (2015, 2017), and the International Roundtable for the Semiotics of Law (2018). I am indebted to the helpful comments and interested ideas I was offered at each setting. My article "Lavascape: Legal Spectacle at Kīlauea" in *Social Semiotics*, published online March 25, 2019, provides a succinct overview of this book.

I have received funding for aspects of this project from the following sources: University of Hawai'i Hilo Research Council's Extramural Proposal Development Award "Coconut Jurisprudence: Law's Marketing of Culture in Hawai'i" in 2014–2015; University of Hawai'i Hilo Social Sciences Division Research Grant "Lava, Legislation, Land" in 2014–2015; University of Hawai'i Hilo Research Council's Research Relations Grant "Eruption, Emergency, and Public Visitation: Comparative Approaches to Lava Tourism in Hawai'i and Iceland" in 2015–2016.

Chapter 1

Fluidity of land, lava, and law

Law books are often thick volumes with dusty pages that are often unread out of fear, but possibly reverence. We are afraid of law for its own distancing from us, for its rigidity. The critique of legal jargon, legalese, or even the historical framework of legal realism would support this. But, is law more fluid than its formal institutionalism might suggest? This book will assert that law must be fluid in order to react and respond to the unstable volcanic environment in Iceland and Hawai'i. Whether in Hawai'i or Iceland, the volcanic environment is geologically active, socially changing, historically evolving, culturally contingent, and of course, legally framed in ways that constantly change. Law can be experienced in a similar manner. Although there aren't "legal tourists" per se, we witness law in a variety of settings, from the court to the street. In the same sense that seeing pictures of the volcano is not the same as actually being at the volcano, observing law may be a different experience than that of direct engaging with it. In other words, going to court is much different than watching court proceedings on television renderings of the courtroom, including such American shows as Judge Judy or the earlier The People's Court. Ironically, and in contrast to visiting the volcano, going to court may be much less dramatic. Watching law happen however, is something that we do in ways that we experience on a daily basis. Similarly, the longer one lives next to the active Kīlauea, the more banal this becomes, especially if the volcano is known to ooze rather than explode. However, even living next to such potentially explosive volcanos such as stratovolcanoes around the world (Mt. Rainer, Mt. Lassen, Mt. Etna, Mt. Fuji, Mt. Pinatubo, and others), is something that people do without worry, except if the lava is flowing towards a populated area.

The perspective of law towards lava is one of formality and distance. Yet, if we consider that we live and breathe law in so many aspects of our everyday lives, then we actually become law. Foucault's premise of governmentality would support this notion of we make law happen by living it in our everyday lives. Yet, ownership of the spectacle can be quite complicated as owning nature, or nature as property, means that such places and activities must first be able to be owned for the public good, and second, able to be exchanged and recognized for possible private ownership. Often, ownership of land is premised upon stability and permanence, as real estate and land tracts do not generally move. Sometimes the move when there is a natural disaster (such as an earthquake that moves the land or buildings upon it, a tornado that wipes out structures, floods or mudslides that sweep away architecture or topsoil, or fires that burn down property). However, in dynamic landscapes, the land itself is on the move with structures subject to the same possible elimination. Regulations of the landscape shift as the landscape itself shifts. Movement is interpreted as change, and change is often not foreseeable; yet through science, we can predict. In contrast thought, law reacts rather than predicts. Law is limited in its foreseeable scope of future events. Yet, law remains a permanent and contested structure of Western social order. Similarly, the permanence of land in the kinetic environment is contestable as property ownership discourses show. On Hawai'i Island, much of the property near the erupting Kīlauea Volcano is privately owned; some is publicly owned by the State of Hawai'i, the County of Hawai'I, or the U.S. government. Here, property ownership designators, such as lines on the earth that delineate who owns what, becomes unclear, even non-existent, in the moving natural landscape. In Hawai'i, land may be covered by lava, and even simply fall into the ocean. In Iceland, the people seem to live on the land and near the spectacle rather than attempting to contain the myriad spectacle that exist in the island nation, including volcanoes, glaciers, geysers, and the seemingly ubiquitous naturally occurring geothermally heated pool, or spa.

This book considers the fluid landscape itself to be a spectacle. Environments of nature coincide with environments of people to reveal a fluidity, or kineticism, of how law works, how law happens, and what law even is in the first place. The mobility of the legal terrain is what keeps law percolating in response to culture, science, tourism. Lava is a legal metaphor for law through its constant oozing and occasional eruption. Similarly, bubbling geysers are a legal metaphor for the intermittent explosiveness of law that is timed and regulated according to a cycle of predicated eruption.

Typically, we see landscapes as stable, as places to be owned or regulated, as fixed architecture, or a built environment that is fixed in meaning. The aesthetics of the stable landscape suggest an absence of movement. Yet, such stability may be an illusion. With the rise of natural events such as rising seas, sinkholes, earthquakes, drought, the landscape is much less stable and more active than first considered. In fact, landscapes that change are spectacles of movement that through their dynamism, affect how law is present in such a landscape. Movements in time, in composition, in approach, and in meaning are movements in which law, through legal perspectivism, is also in motion. The kineticism of land and law reminds us that the dynamic landscape is all around in a variety of contexts. The two contexts explored by this book, the Strokkur Geyser of Iceland and Kīlauea Volcano of Hawai'i, reveal the fluidity or land, lava, and law.

The dynamic landscape

In 1916, Hawai'i Volcanoes National Park (HVNP) on Hawai'i Island was organized and signed into law by U.S. President Woodrow Wilson. Over one hundred years later, over 2.5 million visitors from all of the world came to visit Kīlauea Volcano in HVNP (State of Hawai'i 2018). Since January 3, 1983, lava has been erupting from Kīlauea's East Rift Zone towards the ocean. Forming what is now known as Pu'u 'Ō'ō volcanic cone, there have been numerous episodes in which lava covered the land and added new land to the island. As a revealing commentary on law's jurisdiction, the lava has erupted outside the boundaries of the national park into the Puna District of Hawai'i Island comprised of rural communities organized into small towns and private housing subdivisions numerous times. By the end of the most recent Leilani eruption in 2018, "lava flows destroyed 215 structures and buried 8.9 miles (14.3 km) of highway with lava as thick as 115 ft. (35 m)" (Hawaiian Volcano Observatory n.d.). During this time, the lava flowed underground in lava tubes, over the ground in visible flows, and in and out of the boundaries of the HVNP. The fissure at Pu'u 'Ō'ō evolved through many stages: crater, cone, fissures, lava lake, collapsed cones, lava fountains, oozing streams of lava over the land emptying into the ocean. In 2014, the village of Pāhoa was threatened with lava inundation as that lava flow came within a half mile from the town center. In 2018, lava erupted in the middle of the residential subdivision of Leilani Estates and covered over seven hundred homes. Kīlauea is one of the world's most active volcano, a reality experienced by the island's nearly 200,000 residents.

In the weeks and months that followed the pivotal 6.9 earthquake of May 4, 2018, the legal spectacle shifted domains. Having disappeared into the earth at Halema'uma'u Crater, the lava reappeared outside the National Park on Kīlauea's southern flanks as erupting vents and fissures. With new lava locations, the jurisdiction of this legal spectacle shifted from the public land of the national park to the contested and privately owned land of two residential subdivisions, Leilani Estates and Lanipuna Gardens.[1] Previously within the HVNP, the glow (Figure 1.1) was publicly accessible to those who entered the park's gates. However, as the glow reemerged as spurting fountains and rivers of molten lava flowing across private homes and backyards towards the ocean, access to the glow was publicly restricted, if not effectively privatized through state and county regulations. Competing understandings of jurisdictions arose over how the glow and the flow should be governed. Once out of the park's boundaries, lava flowed uninhibited over layered jurisdictions with a range of jurisdictional actors, including perhaps the most prominent, Madame Pele, the Hawaiian Goddess of Fire [also called *Tutu* (Hawaiian for grandmother) Pele]. Local governing agencies seemed respectful of Madame Pele's power to transform the landscape yet fearful of uncontrolled human viewing as the National Guard manned

Figure 1.1 Glow from Halema'uma'u Crater, Kīlauea Volcano at Hawai'i Volcanoes National Park (March 2013); image available at https://commons.wikimedia.org/wiki/File:Halemaumau_Crater,_March_2013.jpg

roadblocks to the neighborhoods to keep out the public and selectively allow in the local, national, and international media.

Nearly halfway around the world is Iceland. Iceland is a volcanic island similar to Hawai'i Island. Both islands display a kinetic landscape, rich with lava eruptions past and present. Both islands are spectacles of nature that are home to thousands of residents while attracting millions of global visitors. As places of spectacle, both islands reveal insight into the relationship between law and place as found in molten lava, subterraneous geothermal energy, or boiling water that spouts from the earth's surface. While lava in Iceland seems to be more removed from direct contact with residential communities as in Hawai'i, the contexts of tourism and comparative legal response to the dynamic landscape provides a rich link of kineticism between the two places. In both places, the role of law in offering an avenue for sightseers compels a closer comparison between these two otherwise similar islands.

Geysers such as Strokkur (Figure 1.2), spas such as the Blue Lagoon, and other geothermal hotspots including the slothlike movement of the continental plates at Thingvellir National Park, provide a compelling juxtaposition between law and culture in these two places. On Iceland, the unstable terrain is off limits in some of the country's national parks, while this dynamic, changing aspect of nature in a volcanic setting is open and unrestricted to the public. This is evident at Strokkur, geothermal spas such as

Figure 1.2 Strokkur Geyser, March 2016, image copyright: this author.

the Blue Lagoon, but also including others, floors in residential homes with geothermal hearing, and even as a source of humor on the side-of-the-road DIY bakeries using the steam's heat to cook banana bread. On Kīlauea, lava was the island's liquid that most recently spouted, as was the case at Fissure 8 where molten lava spouted nearly 200 ft. in the air during the Leilani eruption of 2018. Here, geothermal energy is outsourced as a private multi-national electricity-generating company rather than the public avenue of heating floors as Iceland as the country's primary source of state-funded heating in homes across the country. Throughout the book, Iceland will be a secondary point of examination with lava from Kīlauea primarily guiding the book's analysis and discussion. In this context of molten lava, pools of boiling water, and the impacts of both on the surrounding environment, the spectacle involves natural phenomenon. As humans, we want to see this events and flock to experience their viewing. We are witnesses to the spectacle of the dynamic landscape. The spectacle also creates a cultural scope in which the natural spectacle creates locally specific reactions, understandings, and ways of living with the spectacle. Ironically, those that live with such natural phenomena may even normalize their everyday frameworks through the relationship with the spectacle. In this way, the spectacle becomes normalized. However, the visitor to such natural phenomena is apart from this cultural normalization. Like any tourist setting, the host culture may welcome or discourage visitation to this spectacle based around the beliefs and practices of ownership, access, and usage.

Home to the spectacle, the kinetic environment is a landscape that moves. This dynamic landscape can include surface features that are themselves in motion, such as glaciers, geysers, or volcanoes. Yet, the dynamic landscape also includes the components of a particular environment, ranging from the air above, related weather, manmade infrastructure, and spontaneous natural occurrences that change the land itself. The materiality of cooled lava is land that was once alive and is now static (Bennett 2010). Yet, before the cooling of lava, the landscape is an enlivened molten terrain that law and culture respond to. Whether in Iceland or in Hawai'i, those of us on the land are subject to what happens beneath the surface. Prediction happens, law responds, and culture adapts and thrives in these kinetic places. As an active and evolving spectacle, Kīlauea and Hawai'i Island, like Iceland, is a dynamic landscape that involves the eruption of magma from the earth's core over the land into the ocean, the explosive movement of rock at the volcano's summit, and the impact that such movement has on the communities, culture, and local governance. The regulation of these places invites a closer look into law itself as a spectacle involving risk, ownership, common sense, and instability. Just as the volcano is a spectacle, law is also a spectacle. Both spectacles are visual, insofar as we see the movement of lava or steam just as we see courts, lawyers, or police officers. We view the spectacle for its superficial character, yet upon closer examination, the dimensions of what we see reveals insights into what really is a landscape or what really does law look like? Landscapes whether natural or legal are dynamic with regard to terrestrial flow and the motion of action framed as public spaces.

Within the context of the most recent turn in the field of legal geography that links spatiality to temporality (Braverman et al., 2014), the dynamic landscape is not fully discussed. Instead, with a focus on the jurisprudence of movement (Barr 2016), the dynamic landscape becomes a kinetic environment that literally expands the time–space relationship of place in order to consider the motion of landscape that make place kinetic and in motion through law and legal frameworks. Such motion invokes spatio-temporality, yet extends the inquiry to frameworks of stability and instability with attention to construction, expectation, and responses to spectacle. This resulting conceptualization of mobility invites a way to see how law works in enlivened terrains. We can experience law's relationship to transition in such everyday mobility frameworks as the road; yet motion also reminds us of the limitations of law with regards to transitions, those same everyday mobility frameworks, and a changing landscape though natural disasters and climate change. Because we are on the move, law must constantly also be on the move. This fluidity of law reminds us that law's relationship to place is constantly in flux and has a difficult time remaining static. In fact, such stability cannot address the evolving terrain that law inhabits, vacates, and returns to within the dynamic landscape. Exploring the changes that accompany place and its occupancy "endeavors to reconnect the concealed, forgotten or prohibited connections between peoples and places, between the human and the more-than-human" as Robyn Bartel (2013, 343) suggests.

In the changing environment of Kīlauea, law's contribution to social order reveals a positionality emerging in multiple ways. Law seems to achieve perceived rationality in times of chaos and jurisdiction even as it is careful *not* to assert complete dominance over an active volcano. The nuance of law's relationship to people within this environment confuses the legal hierarchy of law over nature while elevating law to a position of asserting authority to direct the actions of people when environments come alive. Danger and risk are rationalized in support of law taking responsibility over the spectacle for purposes of public protection. While this often is for public benefit, because the volcanic landscape is an uncontrolled environment and such environments are dynamic and ultimately unresponsive to human authority, law can only control the discursive framing of the spectacle at hand through limiting people's movements and access. Through discursive practice, the law positions itself as the director of management efforts and as the source of control, a responsibility taken out of the hands of the public.

Yet, just as we know that nature is beyond regulation, law is also imperfect in its attempt to control chaos. Chaos, or the discursive antithesis to order and regulation, is fleeting, spontaneous, often without forethought, and happens in everyday scenarios that themselves are beyond regulation. Chaos can transpire in dynamic natural environments such as Kīlauea as well as in manmade environments. Responses to chaos arise in human nature in ways similar to the unpredictability of the enlivened landscape as actions that cannot always so easily be predicted. In considering the chaos of the oozing volcanic landscape of Kīlauea, the lavascape emerges as a place in which order is framed against the backdrop of disorder and articulated through a variety of legal understandings and practices that perpetuate ensuing chaos.

Reading the kinetic landscape of Kīlauea as a lavascape pays particular attention to the complexity of this particular lawscape. Multiple spatialities that reveal law's own conceptualization of its role in this instable environment are evident. Here, the complexities of law are multiple and involve the following interfaces: Legal spectacle; legal materiality; legal imagination; legal semiotics; legal topology. As a visual spectacle within this fluid legal environment, the lavascape of Kīlauea represents a paradox of legality and jurisdictional space involving the post-colonial attempts to corral an active volcano, the Americanized understanding of property and owning nature, and a local culture steeped in indigenous knowledge and practice. In the sections that follow, the legal spectacle of the lavascape at Kīlauea will be examined against the backdrop of a jurisdictional juxtapositioning of order with chaos while critically examining the context of regulation in a kinetic environment characterized by sightseeing, access, and mapping.

Many scholars have envisioned a variety of ways to depict the legal landscape. From the perspectives of those who walk (Barr 2016; Blomley 2011), those who drive (Wagner 2006; Marusek 2016), and those who build buildings (Dovey 1999), zoos (Braverman 2012) or construct walls (Jones 2012; De León 2015), approaches to environments enriched with legal meaning, or what I refer to in this paper as "lawscapes," generate a multi-layered scope of the constitutive relationship between law and everyday life. Andreas Philippopoulos-Mihalopoulos (2015, 4) describes the lawscape as "the way the ontological tautology between law and space unfolds as difference" in ways that are both visible and invisible. John Brigham (2009a, 382) considers the visual framework of the lawscape through lines and explains "seeing jurisdiction means seeing the lines laid out by law and knowing what they mean." Margaret Davies (2017, 30) describes the lawscape insofar as "law becomes *what* it is, *where* it is - in material locations as performed in and by subjects who are both recipients of law and conveyors of it." A theme of law and place that emerges from these varied, yet related characterizations of the lawscape perpetuates the space of law as an ongoing, fluid project of legibility in which the contest of legal authority contrasts with a localized understanding of place.

Because the experience of place is locally determined, ontological frameworks of place reflect the construction of place as a site for events to transpire in certain ways. Whether on the street (Valverde 2012; Marusek and Brigham 2017; Kohn 2004; Blomley 2011) or in the lavascape, understandings of place are framed through law, socio-legal norms and legal regulations. This understanding of place is uniquely emphasized at Kīlauea, as local law currently operates in response to Madame Pele rather than against her. However, this wasn't always the case, as the volcanic flow of lava from neighboring Mauna Loa was bombed by the U.S. military under General George S. Patton in 1935 and again in 1942 in order to literally, arrest the flow of lava (Chiu 2018) while controlling its movement. While the lava did stop, the likelihood of naturally occurring coincidence trumped those foolhardy actions taken by man. Not surprisingly, volcanoes usually have the upper hand against man, and despite renewed calls to bomb Kīlauea in the 2014 Pāhoa flow, local law officials realized that Pele indeed has the right of way on Hawai'i Island. Furthermore, the act of bombing was a cultural affront to Madame Pele, the locally respected Hawaiian deity, and represented a political burden for local lawmakers, many of whom consider Hawai'i to be their home for multiple generations. Therefore, the positionality of law is uniquely determined to be in response to local cultural practice in which Madame Pele represents not only cultural relevance but also a signifier of the natural environment. In Iceland, the eruption of Heimaey of 1973 resulted in the pumping of sea water to cool the lava. Whether the pumping successful stopped the flow of lava or the lava stopped its own is debated (Einarsson 1974), man (and law) is subject to the whims of nature.

Yet, law attempts to skirt both domains, namely that of instilling order while balancing control of a legal spectacle that is nature itself.

Landscape, or in the context of this book, lavascape, is more than just land but also includes air, what's in/under the ground that we don't see, as well as the surface of the ground that we do see. Yet, lava, which is both in/under/on the ground, is a source of continual activity in relationship with local communities and their subsequent legal responses and challenges. In considering this complexity, the focus of this book is the dynamic lava-based landscape as it creates, sustains, and challenges the evolving relationship between law and place. As an innovative, yet underdeveloped area within the field of legal geography, the book adds to the foundational publications of legal geography (Blomley et al. 2001) that have recently evolved with increased attention to the emerging trend of temporality (Braverman et al. 2014) and spatiality (Braverman 2012; Philippopoulos-Mihalopoulos 2015). Movement is the conjunction of space and time in which the action of motion sculpts human relationships with their environment. Neither landscape nor law are consistently stable. Critical engagement with instability provides fluid avenues for interpretation and perspective. Metaphorically, if a related perspective is such that law is distant and as dangerous as molten lava, then law itself becomes free either from challenge, or from direct engagement. Yet, like lava, we are constantly engaged with its development and confronting its evolution.

On Hawai'i Island, there are those who do directly engage with the lava. Be they geologists, university students, or even the public (even those curious ones who stick golf clubs into the lava), the lava invites engagement. However, to engage happens in a variety of ways: from the criminal, to the colloquial, to the sacred. While some disagree (cultural perspective that law is Pele and therefore should be sacred and free from tampering), lava, if touched in the proper manner, can promote the course of scientific study or satisfy human curiosity. In the same way, engaging with the law may be more playful (Brigham 2009, Patricia's article on the playground) than hazardous. Just as lava invites different responses, lava is also a spectacle of modern legality that transforms the lawscape (Philippopoulos-Mihalopoulos 2018) and the nomosphere (Delaney 2010). Whether in Hawai'i, Iceland, or elsewhere, shifting terrains enliven the study of law. Mobility actively engages law through moving vistas, transgressive boundaries, and kinetic materialities. Notions and practices of regulation, order, and governance are perpetually in motion.

Lavascape

The Dynamic Landscape: Legal Geography of (in) Motion examines law's fluidity in environments characterized by movement. In such environments, natural upheavals (landslides, active volcanoes, and melting glaciers) challenge the presumed immutability of manmade milieus (vehicular roadways, built architecture, and designated conservation areas). With land as legal metaphor, law is fluid in its successful social design of an ordered environment. In its material response to transformative environments such on those on Hawai'i Island or in Iceland, law within these dynamic landscapes complicate normative conceptualizations of property, nature, and human positionality of control. Conceptualizations of control challenge static notions of place and expectation associated with the stability of law. Lava is a spectacle, and in response to kinetic environments, so is law. The constant flow of an active volcano results in the production of spectacle. Law seeks to manage this spectacle either through national parks or emergency frameworks by determining risk and hazard in accordance with predictability. While the natural spectacle is fluid in its eruption (lava) or associated bubbling (geothermal), emergency responses to spectacle are themselves fluid types of law that evolve as spectacles transpire. The spectacle of landscape change is a natural phenomenon, but also legal in implicating jurisdictional and cultural fluctuation. Creating legal boundaries around such dynamic places is an attempt by law to contain and preserve this land as public. We can see this in volcanic areas (such as Hawai'i and Iceland) in which national parks become methods of land management that normalize hazards associated with volcanic and geothermal spectacle. We can also see this in the tourist experience in visiting these governed places as well as an interpretive methodological approach to the relationship of law and place. Yet, the concept of public is much more complex than the binary of private/public would otherwise signify.

The landscape in motion is not only a metaphor for law and culture, it represents the fluid relationship between the two. Law is on the move, even when it's grounded. The grounding of law is law's expectations for its own existence and through its existence, the understanding (as well as contestation) of rules and orders through local culture. Such expectations include compliance, continuation (through legal education and lawyering), and operationalization (as in courts). However, law isn't always in control, as the governing practices toward the spectacle attest. Through the reactions and responses to land in motion, we can see how law works as well as its limitations. Law is often *not law* (in the formal sense) and operates through non-legal means that include common sense (although this cannot be essentialized nor presumed to be uniform); accessibility, response to risk frameworks, control through ownership avenues and interpretations as property. For example, do lawyers own law? What about judges? Don't we all effectively "own" law by implementing it uniquely and often unpredictably in our own everyday lives? Through the dynamic movement of everyday life at the spectacle, with its fleeting spontaneity, law is enlivened and ultimately beyond its own control.

In Hawai'i and Iceland, scientific and cultural directives illuminate the boundaries of law as order, jurisdiction attempt to manage the impossible (such as stopping the flow of molten lava or capping live geysers). The known, but often unmanaged aspects to these places draw broader implications about the degree of kineticism inherent to all landscapes that changes how we conceive of and practice law. Through common sense, governance happens in everyday environments. Through tourist accessibility, law witnesses the spectacle. Through frameworks of human risk within the natural environment, law's responsibility is challenged through the (un)predictability of the scientific and natural environment. Through property ownership over nature, law is implicated in control over the spectacle by private as well as public forces. Finally, through overtly non-legal avenues if science, culture, and tourism, law itself is a spectacle within the kinetic environment of the everyday.

The flow of land and sea, geysers, the Icelandic hot pond, the witnessing of molten lava as well as its hardening generate innovative jurisprudential questions focused around temporality, spatiality, and movement (Braverman et al. 2014; Barr 2016). The legality generated by dynamic landscapes further challenges Western, particularly American standards pertaining to environmental management, land ownership, and jurisdiction. Additionally, the spatio-temporality of a landscape in motion raises important questions legal reasoning that jurisprudentially shapes property discourse and related outcomes. Grounded within the field of legal geography, this book contributes to larger questions about epistemologies of property, regulation, and ownership in public environments. Moreover, the book expands conventional assumptions held in the field of legal geography about the stability of landscapes and the fluidity of law. Throughout the book, I consider the movement of lava using a multilayered methodological framework involving messiness (Law 2004), interpretive research design through built space (Yanow and Schwartz-Shea 2006; Dovey 1999), materiality (Brigham 2009b) and landscape (Braverman 2012; Bartel et al. 2013; Barr 2016). Interpretive methodological tools used will include participant observation, contemporary scholarship, newspapers, archival research, judicial doctrine, and case law in order to explore and examine stages of movement that characterize lava (molten, cooled, and hardened) and describe the larger picture of the dynamic landscape.

As part of this interpretive framework, I will examine the contemporary as well as historical contributions of local administrative statutes involving flowing lava, accretion, and public access to lava found in the United States, the State of Hawai'i, the County of Hawai'i, the former Kingdom of Hawai'i, the former Territory of Hawaii, and Iceland. Additionally, I will examine those statutes that govern human entry into the natural environment, such as in Iceland. For example, what does the law say about driving on a glacier? Or, sticking objects into streams of molten lava? Or, even going out to see rivers of lava or to walk on lava once hardened? I will research such questions as what does the law say about rebuilding on land that is owned by private individuals but that has been covered by hardened lava. How does this phenomenon of accretion conflate law with nature in a dynamic and kinetic fashion? Does the law really have a say about everything? Who owns new lava? What happens when the law is silent? Through these various ordinances and governing structures, I hope to better answer the larger questions of the book, that include: What does it mean to access the spectacle? How is the spectacle materialized through local ordinances and national guidelines? How do human institutions that seek to manage nature tell us about the fluidity of law and legality in environments that cannot be contained?

In chapter one "Fluidity of Land, Lava, and Law," stable landscapes will be considered alongside dynamic landscapes. In the resulting lavascape, governance in the form of lava zone mapping and responses to recent Kīlauea lava flows reflect law's ability to conflate the present with the future while also accounting for the past. Time happens according to the earth's clock, which speeds up or oozes without pronouncement or regularity. Time also happens according to the human clock involving years, months, and days. As the most recent (and current) eruption of Kīleau has been ongoing since 1983, the chronology of events and legal responses shaped by those events can be mapped as part of the discourse of territoriality. Evident in the flow of the lavascape, law itself can be mapped according to its responses and reactions which are fluid in nature and transpire in myriad ways. As a motile agent, lava on the move ultimately dictates the tone for law's ability to govern and respond to locally responsive cultural frameworks of order, authority, and resistance. Resistance to law's whims may even be as consistently reliable as the resistance of lava to barriers erected to contain the flow. Even evident through the restriction of access to its flow, or calls to bomb lava on the move, law's turf is ultimately governed by nature. One might ask, when does Tutu Pele ever *not* have the right of way, or rather, when does lava obey the law? *Never.* And, when does the law obey lava? *Always.*

Methodologically, the study of law and place in conjunction with motion can be messy (Law and Singleton 2005; Law 2004) and subject to whimsy untamable through strict data collection or expected patterns, particularly when considering the multifaceted textures of everyday life (Law 2004). This phenomenon of messiness is counter to traditionally defined sets of variables or data sets, which are tidy and neat. In dynamic landscapes, law responds to natural phenomenon in such a way that neat and tidy is not possible and is constantly challenged by nature itself. Similarly, the jurisdictional framing of natural phenomena by a variety of regulatory measures characterizes the limitations of law within the kinetic setting of natural spectacle. Additionally, law is constitutively framed by contextualized, locally specific cultural ways of knowing, enacting, and resisting forms of regulation that sculpt human understanding with natural phenomena.

Because the spectacle is a visual phenomenon, I will be drawing upon an interpretive methodological framework that frames the image of the kinetic environment against a material backdrop of interaction with natural phenomenon. Such interaction becomes a multilayered spectacle involving the kinetic approach not only regarding the natural environment, but also about how it is framed, accessed, described, viewed, and governed. Kinetically, these interactions are fluid and constantly shifting and through an interpretive approach, this fluidity, while messy (Law 2004) is also a spectacle in which law happens while volcanoes ooze and geysers erupt. Legalizing the spectacle is an amalgamation of many factors and dynamic influences that includes tourism, policy, semiotics, and cultural engagement. Each of these contributing angles reveals important areas of empirical evidence that reference and describe the spectacle in its natural and legal forms. I draw upon the interpretive research design methodology of Dvora Yanow and Peregrine Schwartz-Shea (2006). Methodological tools I have used include participant observation, policies and statutes, interviewing, archival research, judicial doctrine and case law, and constitutive legal examples of cultural engagement.

If we further consider the idea of the spectacle using law and the metaphorical foundation of accessibility, ownership, phenomenon, and normalization, law is a spectacle in which access, definition, control, risk, management, and visitation each exist and shape our understanding of what law is and how it works. Is law beyond our control? Yes and no. As the constitutive approach to law suggests, law and culture constitute one another. Culture ebbs and flows as styles and expectations change; similarly, law ebbs and flows, often with the speed of law moving painfully slow. However, law can speed up, often without warning (and can be compared to the metaphor of the unpredictability of nature). In courts, law is less dynamic engaged perhaps, often tied up for months, even years. However, on the streets, law is motive and more likely to respond to immediate change. Often, the law is violent, as suggested by Robert Cover (Minow et al., 1995), and is similar to the unforeseen explosiveness of lava or the lava delta shelves that break off into the ocean without warning. As an aspect of formal law, the courts invite us (the public) for viewing, for visitation to the spectacle of a trial. However, often, that public visibility is closed off, as many arrests draw attention to. Law is visible, yet often in visible. Law responds, but often ignores stimuli. Such stimuli might include political movements (that call for immediate change, cultural changes (such as marriage equality), or scientific advancement (consider stem cell research). Courts are spectacles. Outside of courts, law often operates through extra-legal ways (such as handicapped parking space and the medical approval needed to receive a legal placard). Law on the street happens in fleeting moments, which are often not recorded; however, with the introduction of the person-based camera, many of these interactions are now visible *and* recorded for later viewing. The spectacle of viewing, whether at the court, on the street, or at the volcano, engenders an understanding of that which is seen, for the ontology of vision is based in the visible, the invisible, and the understood. Unpacking this later aspect of vision, or deconstructing the status quo, is how we come to see the landscape of law in the kineticism of the dynamic environment.

In chapter two "Epistemologies of Jurisdiction," the quiet, bubbling, glowing environment of lava is explored through indigenous knowledge of the spectacle against the backdrop of the illusory containment of lava and law's management of the untamed spectacle. People come to watch the spectacle. To witness the color and awe of molten lava is simply extraordinary. To manage access to the spectacle, law serves to visually regulate the view as well as to control access to the spectacle itself. National parks and areas of legal reserve are created to protect the spectacle as well as people from the spectacle. Yet, ownership of the earth (Linklater 2013) is the paradox of stewardship over the environment to a colonizing presence over nature itself (Spence 1999). Law engages in a relationship with scientific prediction and study of the spectacle and results in legal frameworks pertaining to risk. Law is a local manager of risk resulting (possibly) from natural events and human interaction with such motive environments. Risk of natural events, such as the eruption of a volcano or spouting of a geyser, is exciting and attracts visitors from all over the world. While risk may be legally managed, control over risk is often beyond law's reach. Through the ownership over nature, law seeks to tame the wildness of the landscape in motion. The management of risk then becomes the management of common sense, as evident in disaster frameworks and emergency proclamations. Common sense is then locally generative, just as law is locally applicable. Common sense is the vision (or backbone) of law, in which governance is facilitated through a shared understanding of what the problems are (and how to solve them).

Visitation for purposes of experiencing spectacle generates with a sense of legal perspectivism in which we witness and experience (even regard with awe) law as a spectacle in the same way – through watching/beholding yet being wary of eruptions, movement, and geyser bubbling from a safe distance. Yet, instability (either in law or in the kinetic environment) never disappears as law's positivist capacity is always in question (as demonstrated by the constitutive relationship between law and place/everyday life) and volcanic environments are active and rumbling. The proximity to an active volcano is one that is risky, yet thrilling. The thrill of being so close generates some of the fear of what might potentially happen, such as perhaps, an active lava eruption. The imaginative play associated with exploding lava seems to be a favorite aspect of childhood games insofar as one is careful not to "step on the lava." Law plays into this game by creating an overlook at which the lava can be viewed at a safe distance. This construction of the lavascape is paradoxical insofar as law limits the reaches of human/volcano interaction, yet imperfectly eliminates the danger. But, what really is danger? Is it the threat of eruption or eruption itself? This chapter examines the creation of the HVNP in the early-twentieth-century Territory of Hawaii through a layering of jurisdiction. This same type of layering also frames the legal phenomenon of accretion, or the building of new land from lava inundation. Within the lavascape, accretion and jurisdiction characterize law's management of the unstable as an illusion of stability in a terrain governed by Tutu Pele.

Chapter three "Legalizing the Spectacle" considers the performance of property on a stage of eruption in which land is conflicted between public and private understandings of ownership and access. Legal perspectivism, or the positioning of law for viewing/interpretation/critique opens up the idea of "where is law"? Austin Sarat (1990) asserts the "law is all over." However, we should question the ubiquitous nature of law, for to be everywhere might in fact be nowhere. At the same time, if law is everywhere (but nowhere at the same time), where might it not be? Law may not be in an active lava flow or in the eruption of an Icelandic geyser. Nonetheless, legal perspectivism reminds us that law is impacted by such natural phenomena and through the movement of the dynamic landscape, is compelled to respond. Why must law get involved? How does law get involved? The spectacle of volcanic activity is rich with science, art, culture, and social aspects. The volcano seems to be free from law, or to maintain a legal perspective in which law's ability to govern and set order is challenged. While volcanic flows or bubbling water are fluid in nature, law is not always so fluid. We see this in the rigidity of the legislative process, the amending of constitutions (particularly the U.S. Constitution), or the formality of courtroom procedure. Yet, the volcano is not without regulation. Experiencing the volcano at Halema'uma'u Crater happens in the National Park at a distance, in a controlled parking lot, and behind fences. Lava is distant and purposely not up close. The crater's glow is managed through entry to the park. The park is federal jurisdiction. The volcano is therefore effectively owned by the U.S. government who accept a fee for its viewing. The viewing is managed in a variety of ways. The flow of land and sea, the migration of people, the building of roads, and even the hardening of molten lava generate innovative jurisprudential questions focused around temporality, spatiality, and movement. As lava flows and geothermal water bubbles, nature assumes a kinetic presence. National parks seek to harness this movement through jurisdictional frameworks. However, nature is not bound to either observe or obey manmade boundaries and often transverses, some might say transgresses, these constructed borders are often perpetuated through private claims of territory and purchase. This chapter examines the public quality of the spectacle as possible disaster, but also as possible hybridized site of law, entrepreneurial culture, and local tourism at official Lava Viewing Areas set up by Hawai'i County Civil Defense Agency at areas outside the HVNP.

Chapter four "Topologies of Governance" considers the ebbs and flows of terrain through maps, zones, and cadastral knowledge of land and law. Land and law are visualized through physical boundaries (rock walls, roadblocks, and gates) but also through the mapping of terrain. Maps are a source of legal regulation insofar as the territory of law predicts movement and usage of land based upon mapped terrains (Scott 1998). The mapping of landscape is further premised upon social and cultural forms of usage and presence. Temporality, terrain, and spectacle affect the mapping of land and the dynamic representation of land over time. Maps are law's attempt to regulate change and manage predictability, particularly in volatile landscapes.

While molten lava is indeed chaotic, with the volcanic environment wild and on fire, law depends upon non-legal actors such as science to interpret the chaos. Even as houses burn, roads split open with the movement of the earth, and the path of the lava seems to be unknown, science predicts the past, present, and future topographical direction of the lava. Through the revised mappings of lava by the United States Geological Survey (USGS), the flow of lava can be consistently predicted with startling accuracy. Initiated by the USGS in 1974, the Lava Zone Map depicts zones of risk as to where the lava is most likely in future eruptions. Using a range from one to nine, the historical precedent for lava flows is mapped according to the topographical contours of the land and previous lava activity. In this way, the mapping of risk according to the past and future reveals a legal discourse for the present. While the future carries risk, the mapping of lava represents a legalized sense of possibilities governing the here and now. Risk is a disciplinary, normalizing institution (O'Malley 2004) that fosters a sense of governmentality that heightens the possibility of threat, particularly in Lava Zone One where Leilani Estates was located. If law is then the manager of threat, then prediction is the avenue of governance that seeks to control rather than simply react and/or respond. In Lava Zone One, the risk of future lava inundation and property loss was high with the legally discursive responsibility towards the eruption of lava perceived as less of a surprise than if it has erupted in other lava zones. Yet, despite the risk of likely lava inundation, many residents built homes in Leilani and Lava Zone One due to the relative affordability of land and property.

Similar to an architecture of risk that pits the local governance against the interests of private real estate, the paving and re-paving of local roads covered by lava flows is an attempt by law to quell the evolving sense of time and place. Once the lava cools, the law can retake control over the environment by rebuilding access. Vehicular access to newly covered lava areas gives a sense of heterotemporality over eruption that benefits the stability of law to maintain order in otherwise disrupted areas. Law's conquest to tame the wildness of the kinetic environment happens every time a road is repaved over once molten lava, evident in the chapter's discussion of the Chain of Craters Road within HVNP. Consequentially, the approach to law is operationalized through a framework of perceived power, as law is situated as the solution to chaos. Through this positioning, a sense of legal perspectivism perpetuates the dichotomy in which law is at odds with a motile landscape. The fluidity of landscape as chaos reveals law to be stuck in the binary between right/wrong, chaos/order, legal/illegal, while ignoring the gray areas that prevail in everyday environments involving law and nature and/or human nature. Behavior of the potentially chaotic is controlled monitored parking lots, roadblocks that maintain vehicular rules and penalties for violation, and even the wandering of those in lava areas as needing to be curbed and contained through military presence.

In chapter five "Knowing the Ropes," the evolving relationship between common sense, risk, and the spectacle is considered from a semiotic perspective that sees risk amidst dimensions of imaginative response to normative frameworks of danger and alternative understandings of common sense. In ways that will be seen in greater detail, teasing the legal spectacle is a testing of law's authority. Lava is normatively constructed as a hazard. Due to its extreme temperature, it would seem to be rational that we should stay far from such a potential danger. And, yet, lava at Kīlauea often oozes rather than explodes. Through scientific prediction and historical accounts of where the lava has flows, law could relax in the knowledge that the natural environment is much more consistent and less potentially chaotic than it is characterized to be. Or, as those familiar with Kīlauea and her history might purport, Madame Pele is just doing what she has done for a very long time. As the creation of the HVNP in the early twentieth century attests, law *over* the volcano in the form of boundaries and gates and subsequent legislation either to protect the landscape from human intrusion or to control unauthorized sightseeing to the spectacle is ultimately challenged and superseded by Madame Pele. Madame Pele predates modern law of the landscape. Similar to the volcanic energy of Kīlauea, geothermal energy of a geyser captures the attention at Iceland's Strokkur Geyser. Similar to the lavascape, this geyserscape provides the semiotic nuance to understanding the ropes and legally "knowing the ropes" literally by looking at the ropes that guard the geyser from the visiting public.

The Concluding Remarks "Jurisprudence of Enlivened Terrain" looks at the kinetic landscape as a legal metaphor for how law really works in the changing environment by considering law's extra-legal/non-legal dependency on actors such as culture and science. If we consider the movement of lava to represent a legal metaphor for order versus chaos, we can see that the spectacle is really law. Law is similar to lava, as both are premised on fluidity and durability as each morphs and moves. Just as lava can take multiple forms ranging from molten to cooled, law itself can take many forms from formal to socio-legal. Law is fluid just like the movement of the environment that we see only timely snippets of. Therefore, what we see is what law wants us to see, namely the stability and the authority to regulate, control, and punish those who violate its directives and jurisdictional sense of control. Law doesn't want us to see its misgivings, namely that law really isn't in control, as evident in the persistence of Lava Loiters, or even in the relaxation of its own directives in which tourists in a boat were injured by spraying lava too close to the shore.

Law regulates through a variety of methods, from limiting access to the image, to the building of roads, to the mapping of hazard-prone areas. Law's method for regulating change and natural spectacle is organized according to government agencies that strive to diagnose and seek solutions to changing terrain. However, in landscapes that are kinetically premised upon motion and movement, legal authority arising from organizations often competes with individual common sense that challenges legal direction. Law ironically hopes we will use our own best judgment, but doesn't seem to fully trust us to make the best choice as arrests, punishment, and controlled access to sites of spectacle routinely occur. Paradoxically, movement and materiality in mobile places challenge law's normative governing capacity in fleeting moments whether in public parks, on private land, visiting an active geyser, or standing near a river of oozing molten lava.

Note

1 Henceforth, I will be referring to these two subdivisions collectively as "Leilani Estates" or "Leilani."

Chapter 2

Epistemologies of jurisdiction

Governing the spectacle at Kīlauea has a history in which law and its consequences on property, place, and people become the source of spectacle. In this chapter, law morphs from an indigenous model of land usage to a Western model of property ownership in different forms with the ownership over the active land changing over time. This conceptual shift, a shift in law's positionality towards the environment, results in the reframing of nature as revered and perpetuating its own domain to a position of legal subjectivity through law's possession. Understandings and practices of land ownership and power shift the epistemologies of jurisdiction from veneration to conservation. Through the formation of the Hawai'i Volcanoes National Park (HVNP), the spectacle of control is the control of spectacle. Kīlauea, once untamed and worshiped as sacred site by Hawaiians, is domesticated through Western law as a federally protected natural reserve. Yet, despite this legal framework of ownership over this volcanic environment, Kīlauea, the home to Pele, Hawaiian goddess of fire, ultimately asserts and reclaims her right of way despite the imposition of manmade boundaries. Pele's right of way, or the ultimately un-owneable flow of lava over the landscape, challenges law's management of the unstable to reveals the illusory containment of law over nature.

Pele's right of way

Historically, within the *ahupua'a* of Kapāpala, the *'ili* (land parcel) of Keauhou is, and was, home to Kīlauea Volcano and the goddess Pele (Maly and Maly 2005). Prior to the arrival of the American system of property which segmented lands into public and privately owned property, the Hawaiian system of land occupancy was built upon the *ahupua'a* in which a land area was created that spanned from *mauka* (the mountains) to *makai* (the ocean) making as much of the natural resources available to native Hawaiians to live. The area of Kīlauea within Keauhou is sacred and generally off limits to most people with the exception of a select few. Those who did pass through the area left offerings and prayer to Pele (Maly and

Maly 2005, 6). This area was also used for travel and footprints that have been preserved at Keonehelelei within the HVNP show that this area was an indigenous site for occasional regional conflict as well as a pathway to traverse the island. These fossilized footprints in an area of volcanic ash were later legally acquired by the HVNP in 1938 (Moniz Nakamura 2003). Following the *Māhele 'Āina* (land division) of 1848, the *'ili* of Keauhou was first awarded to Chiefess Victoria Kamāmalu, a granddaughter of Kamehameha I, founder of the Kingdom of Hawai'i (Maly and Maly 2005). Governed by the *ali'i*, or Hawaiian royalty who leased the land for ranching ungulates (cattle and goats) and the harvesting of local flora (native woods such as Koa and native plants including the fibers of the *hāpu'u* (tree fern) (Maly and Maly 2005).

Additionally, from 1823 to the mid 1830s, religious practitioners would stay on the land to honor the *kapu* (traditional laws and customs) associated with Pele and her worship, which included the depositing of remains of the deceased at the volcano (Maly and Maly 2005, 7).

Additionally, during this timeframe (1840s until 1916), the Volcano House was developed as a site that provided meals and accommodations as well as guided tours by native Hawaiians of Kīlauea Volcano. These temporary facilities for visitor lodging at the rim of the volcano were constructed as early as 1840 (Maly and Maly 2005, 6) and seemed to follow increased visitation to the area since the arrival of the first foreigners to Kīlauea in the company of Hawaiians (Maly and Maly 2005, 7). In 1863, the lease of Keauhou was granted by Chiefess Kamāmalu and her father, M. Kekūanao'a of Oahu to F.B. Swain, a rancher from Ka'ū. The lease, which excluded the fisheries and Koa trees as well as the *kuleana* (responsibility, well-being) of residents of Keauhou, was initially for a period of three years for $80 per year after which tenancy could be continued (Maly and Maly 2005, 277). By 1865, the lease transferred to C.E. Richardson and his associates Reed, Jones, and Kaina, who built the original Volcano House in 1877, which was a structure of mixed Hawaiian and Western architecture (Maly and Maly 2005, 7). Following the 1893 overthrow of Queen Lili'uokalani, crown lands previously owned by the *ali'i*, including those of Kīlauea, were ceded to the American territorial government of Hawai'i under the jurisdiction of the U.S. Congress until Hawaiian Statehood in 1959.

Although the *ali'i* technically owned Kīlauea, the American quest for ownership over the spectacle was managed in a quite different way, namely through the jurisdiction of the national park. Yet, despite legal frameworks of land ownership and conservation management, Madame Pele ultimately exercises her right of way, meaning that despite law's attempts to control the volcanic landscape, lava will ultimately choose its own path and erect its own boundaries. Materially speaking, once the activity subsides and lava cools, black rock remains. The cooled lava terrain is a newfound form of land that becomes property, once it is fully hardened. Whether the property is in the public domain, such as in the National Park, or in private hands of homeowners in contemporary Puna subdivisions, management of the lava is a literally, a heated topic. Throughout recent history, Kīlauea has covered numerous towns, villages, residential subdivisions, and other aspects of the manmade landscape. Locally, this continual cycle of landscape change is culturally referred to as Pele "cleaning house", as the landscape is wiped clean of trees, structures, vehicles, and other manmade aspects of a lived environment. The recognition is clear that Pele is in control of this land and asserts that nature is controlled by nature.

For law, jurisdiction lays the foundation for ownership. Jurisdiction of land considered "spectacle" suggests conceptualizations of law that form the relationship between people and terrain. At Kīlauea, the conquest of the spectacle was used to frame the terrain as *terra incognita*, or as land that was otherwise unoccupied and "empty" and devoid of law. Law in this sense was Western in scope and did not give credence to the already existent Hawaiian governance of this wild terrain through the *ahupua'a*. This Westernized, Americanized legal perspective was contextualized by similar land conquests in places interpreted to be devoid of people, or of people that mattered to law at the time (Weiner 2006; Spence 1999). This selective colonization of the lavascape via the formation of the HVNP reflected the conquering prowess of law that generated the public quality of volcano as a govern-able spectacle and was typical of American expansionism in the late nineteenth/early twentieth century.

Foreign influences shaped legal jurisdiction and cultural usage of the volcano from that of a sacred place to a place best suited for foreign visitation. In 1911, American journalist Alexander Hume Ford asserted in the "Editorial Comment" of *The Mid-Pacific Magazine*, Territory of Hawai'i, that Kīlauea is the "acme of all that is sublime and wonderful in Hawaii."[1] Ford writes that "Hawaii is the world's wonderland" and Kīlauea National Park "should be the park of the people." However, the "people" Ford is referring to are the people who arrive to the Islands as visitors to the island, as he heralds that "Hawaii is a summer and winter resort." Describing accessibility to the public spectacle, Ford further states "Access to the park should be made accessible to the man of humblest means as well as to the man with an auto. There is no reason why a railway should not traverse this proposed park." Yet, even as early as 1847, King Kamehameha III commissioned the Government Road System (Maly and Maly 2005, 267) that would be based upon the strengthening of pre-existing trails. In the words of George L. Kapeau, Governor of the Island of Hawai'i to the Minister of the Interior, Keoni Ana in 1847, "If the roads are put into proper condition, there are a lot of places for the strangers to visit when they come here" (Maly and Maly 2005, 268). Jurisdiction over the spectacle is in this case making sure that the spectacle is accessible to the visiting public.

Ford was excited about Kīlauea, as it is one of the "seven superlative scenic Wonders of the World" that existed in the Territory of Hawai'i, a recently acquired American jurisdiction. Kīlauea is also the "largest and safest active volcano in the world," according to Ford. "Let us have a National Park that is really a park for all the people all the time. Kīlauea belongs to the Nation. It is her great scenic asset; the Nation should care for the volcano, and it will," further asserted Ford. At that time, Hawai'i was the Territory of Hawaii under the United States, with the "nation" being the U.S. and the "people" presumably meaning Americans rather than Hawaiians. Through the language of "winter and summer resort" and "visitors arriving to the Islands," Kīlauea was heralded as an American treasure owned and cared for by the U.S. government and shared with "people," both native and foreign, through the development of roads (even a railway) and contemporaneous gating of the volcano through the Park's boundaries. At the time and even in the present day, Western law presumes that access to this "safe" volcano and legalized spectacle was otherwise not ensured unless the U.S. assumed not only stewardship, but ownership over this wild terrain.

Law's management of the unstable

In 1911, the Hawaii[2] Volcano Research Association was formally established on the crater's rim by American geologist Thomas Jaggar and his financier, Lorrin A. Thurston, an American attorney from Honolulu (Moniz Nakamura 2010, 5). Three years later, the Hawaiian Volcano Observatory (HVO) was constructed. In 1916, Hawaii National Park was established (Moniz Nakamura 2010, 1). The present-day Jaggar Museum, built in 1985, is located at the site of the original building dedicated to Jaggar's thirty years studying Kīlauea. In May 2018, following the continuous, nearly daily explosions at the summit that resulted in the partial collapse of the caldera, Jaggar Museum was closed to the public.

The pragmatics of containing a volcano within a stated jurisdiction, whether for research or for visitation, is a function of legal formalism over nature. It is this formalism that invites further discussion into law as a justified colonizer of nature through the auspices of public safety and environmental protectionism. In her extensive work on zoos, legal scholar Irus Braverman (2012) describes the legally constructed gaze of viewing wild animals in a zoo setting through the regulatory structure of the Association of Zoos and Aquariums (AZA). Braverman sees such a zoo setting as a visual dynamic in which observations are managed and nature is constructed as sanitized. Animals are viewed as wild, yet paradoxically also as tamed through the construction of their surroundings. Braverman (2012, 62) argues that zoos have become "pedagogical institutions" tasked with the responsibility of saving nature.

Through the creation of the HVNP, a similar dynamic seeks to regulate, if not tame, the wild creature that is Pele, living deep within Kīlauea's caldera. The establishment of the Park in the 1900s by the American territorial government was to tame the animalistic tendencies of an active volcano. Just as zoos cordon off nature through zooptic viewing and foster a Benthamatic panopticonic approach to seeing nature, the HVNP cordoned off the wildness of the lava at Halema'uma'u Crater volcano for purposes of *in sita* conservation, or the care of nature in the wild. Prior to the eruption of 2018, visitors were allowed to view the glow from a distance with narrative displays and a viewing platform monitored by the Park's governance at Jaggar Museum's overlook at Halema'uma'u Crater. Such a comparison is helpful in understanding the Park's approach to keeping the glow under observation and making it visible and seemingly under control through a sanitized and distant viewing area. Just as a tiger may be more approachable from the other side of her enclosure fence, glowing lava seems much more picturesque, more tamed, and less wild from the overlook and under the pastoral watch of the Park.

In considering Alexander Hume Ford's earlier perspective of pastoral care over the wildness of nature, the HVNP was proposed by Congress at the same time as other newly formed national parks: Yellowstone (Wyoming), Yosemite (California), Crater Lake (Oregon), Mount Rainer (Washington), Hot Springs (Arkansas), and Glacier (Montana). According to Lorrin A. Thurston, Secretary for the Trail and Mountain Club of Hawai'i in March 1911:

> an examination of the several National Park reservations shows that a reservation is made chiefly by reason of some unusual or interesting natural phenomena or some grand or varied natural scenery, so unique or important as to remove it from purely local interest and make it a subject of national importance, which should be preserved for and made accessible to the people of the entire nation.

Thurston, a politician who advocated American annexation of the Kingdom of Hawai'i, was later credited with the naming of the Thurston Lava Tube in the HVNP, a popular cavernous walk-through formed by previously active rivers of lava flowing underground. Thurston saw Kīlauea as a national treasure in this U.S. Territory (1898–1959) and wanted to have this "natural phenomenon" under American rather than Hawaiian control. His justification of legalizing this spectacle was the government-ensured "neutralizing" of nature for purposes of public access and scientific study to help in earthquake prediction around the world. Thurston (1911, 320) argued that public control of this spectacle was "necessary" to guard against the potential limitations from private ownership (road tolls, possible restrictions of access) of the volcano. Thurston (1911, 320) noted "the spirit of commercialism has not yet reached Hawaii, to the extent of fencing in the volcano and charging a quarter for admission, as was formerly done at Niagara, before it became public property; but civilization is advancing in the Pacific and the possibility exists." Yet, perhaps ironically, the spirit of commercialism is alive and well in the present day at the Park where a gate with entry fees has been established and maintained by the National Park Service at Kīlauea, as well as expensive gift shops, and upscale dining and lodging. Even prior to the formal establishment of the HVNP, Hawaiian *ali'i* engaged in some commercial land transactions, such as the lease of Keauhou from Kamāmalu to Swain.

The national treasure of Kīlauea of contemporary America that is found in the HVNP exists in a pragmatic paradox (Richland 2007) with indigenous Hawaiian practice and American law. Through legal protections, visitors to the park who arrive to worship Pele are excused from paying the entry fee. This practice is the paradoxically neutralizing presence of Western law in protecting the free exercise of religion as guaranteed by the First Amendment of the U.S. Constitution for the religious practice of Native Hawaiians. Access and ability for religious practice on federally owned land is legally acknowledged and culturally protected. Offerings to Pele, the Hawaiian goddess of fire, are routinely placed at the crater's rim, while chants (*oli*) can be heard, or hula is danced. Religious workshop of Pele as protected by U.S. law is the legal/cultural hybridization of religious freedom with natural conservation. The rights of other religious groups, such as Jehovah Witnesses, to practice their faith within the Park are also protected. In terms of worshipping Pele, this hybridization of American and indigenous law is place-based and in response to local cultural and religious practice that predated Western law and continues to sustain the local relationship to Kīlauea. Yet, this relationship is by no means impervious to critique, as the effect of the legal regulation of culture as spectacle is nonetheless controlled through Western law while tempering indigenous self-determination over the spectacle (Marusek 2014). Nature under American jurisdiction is often legally restricted as the legal management and control over access to environment and its features frames Native American religious rituals on the mainland United States and Native Alaskan practices in Alaska just as it restricts the worship of Pele within the setting of a federally controlled National Park setting.

However, even more of a paradox exists in the semiotic of Pele herself, as Pele is a representative symbol of the national park, as depicted in the National Park Service's website image below (Figure 2.1), a jurisdiction that is constructed by Western law. Yet, the paradox is pragmatic, as suggested by Justin Richland (2007) in considering that depictions of Pele remind visitors (as well as the park authorities) of the historic framing of Kīlauea as uniquely Hawaiian in origin.

Yet, the paradox is incomplete when considering the law's conquest of Kīlauea through the concept of *terra incognita*. Thurston (1911, 320) described the lack of roads to and at the volcano as problematic "as it must be remembered that a large part of the adjacent volcanic wonders are located in a tropical forest jungle, with few roads, or even paths, so that many objects and points of the most intense interest are not only now

Figure 2.1 Visitors admiring restored Herb Kane mural; available at https://www.nps.gov/havo/learn/news/20150921_pr_kane.htm

inaccessible by are practically unknown." The view that Territorial Hawai'i was a wilderness needing taming was typical of racist American imperialism in the nineteenth and twentieth centuries (Immerwahr 2019). Thurston dismissed the validity of local ownership and/or usage of this place as well as the existence of local knowledge, either historical or at the time of writing at the turn of the twentieth century. In this way, Thurston reminds us that the spectacle of Kīlauea as territory was legitimized through legal domination of both place and people for the purposes of public ownership and U.S. control. In this way, that which is "public" is really only selectively so, as the ultimate determination of control rests with the elite few. With such confounding arrogance, Thurston (1911, 324) asserted:

> Those who are chiefly interested in, who come to see the volcanoes named, are not the people of Hawaii. Thousands of them have never seen the volcanoes and hardly know that they exist. The interested ones are Americans from the mainland and scientists and tourists from the entire world. Unless the region described comes under Federal control the greater part of it will remain for years to come the terra incognita that it now is.

Thurston not only territorialized the actual spectacle but also tried to claim the epistemology of the spectacle as uniquely American. By advocating the "unknown" nature of Kīlauea, local and indigenous Hawaiian knowledge frameworks of Kīlauea were colonized in similar manner to the overthrow of the Kingdom of Hawai'i. Native epistemologies about Kīlauea were supplanted with an Americanized knowledge about volcanoes and their contributions to science and tourism that did not include reference to indigenous relationships to life on an active volcano until later in the twentieth century. Devoid of this epistemological foundations, increased American access to Kīlauea via the construction of roads and even railroads can be interpreted as a legal metaphor for colonizing nature. Literally, Thurston (1911, 332) presumed he had paved the way for an Americanized claiming of this kinetic frontier as he states:

> The proposed Hawaiian National Park is a natural wonderland. It is such a combination of remarkable volcanic phenomena, climactic contrasts and botanical variety as exists nowhere else in the world, and such as it is scarcely believable could co-exist in so limited an area were it not attested by overwhelming evidence. By right of preeminent fitness, it should be taken into the control of the national government, to be preserved and protected for all time as a beauty spot, a health resort, a geological museum, a botanical garden, and a station for scientific study of the problems of world building, of volcanic action and the cause of earthquakes, for the benefit of the entire American nation and the people of all the world.

Walter F. Frear (1911), Governor of Hawai'i, heralded Thurston's justification for American entitlement at this sacred place by arguing: "Much of these areas is public land, and the remainder can be obtained at little cost. There is a hotel at Kīlauea, on the road that encircles the island; and there has recently been constructed a scenic road from this hotel to the lake of fire in the crater. Additional roads are needed to make other wonders accessible." The possibility of tourism for a globally public viewing generates the legal articulation of possession over this spectacle as American continues the westward expansion of its national borders (Maly and Maly 2005; Immerwahr 2019). Thomas A. Jaggar (1916), the then-Director of the Hawaiian Volcano Observatory, further states, "the Hawaiian volcanoes are truly a national asset, wholly unique of their kind, the most famous in the world of science and continuously, variously and harmlessly active volcanoes on earth." Paradoxically, the perceived safety of this place is juxtaposed against the desire to own land that is wildly active and worshipped by local indigenous people in what was formerly the Kingdom of Hawai'i. It is this contradiction which positions this wilderness, as well as the land and its people, as ripe for American ownership and legal domination. Moreover, the consideration of Kīlauea as "harmlessly active" is another facet of a colonizing mindset that seeks authority and domination over nature.

As noted previously, the HVNP was created from formerly Kingdom lands and leased to private individuals by the *ali'i*. Later these lands were bought by the U.S. Department of the Interior. These lands were also acquired through Executive Orders, such as Executive Order No. 83 (Nov. 6, 1920) "Setting Aside Land for Public Purposes" or seized for purposes of "public protection." However, rather than a perhaps more contemporary application of public safety involving the threat of bodily harm, this notion of protecting the public transpired through governmental ownership over the volcano for purposes of tourism and visitation. In this way, harm was contextualized through immediate access to the spectacle and the perceived lack of legal control over its accessibility. However, through the creation of the HVNP by the Department of the Interior, control over this land was ensured by the federal government. As such, the ultimate jurisdiction of this site was removed from local governance and indigenous populations. Legal ownership of this volcanic spectacle sets the stage for the larger legal narrative of safety and calm that is threatened if American control is absent. This narrative of taming the natural environment extended beyond land, to local people and Native Hawaiian ownership of the land under the Kingdom and later territorial American government. The territorialization of the spectacle, especially as the spectacle was considered safe, rationalized the impetus for the colonization of the wild and unstable terrain of Kīlauea. Dominance over nature was represented through an extended national jurisdiction over the spectacle of molten lava, geologic instability, and indigeneity at the volcano. Control over the land, symbolized in the creation of a national park, fostered a narrowed sense of public to limit Hawaiian presence, heighten American presence, and increased foreign presence to attract visitors from all over the world. This definition of the public perpetuated the seeming justification of control through American jurisdiction over a tamed site of natural wonder.

As legalized spectacle, Kīlauea and the indigenous Hawaiians were denied agency through ownership by American territorial jurisdictional pronouncement as access to the spectacle was restricted in ways similar to other national parks created and administered by the U.S. Department of Interior (Spence 1999). Law's dynamic force attempting to contain the kinetic landscape, whether that landscape includes active volcanoes in Hawai'i, Wyoming (Yellowstone), or elsewhere in the country. Owning nature is the postcolonial legacy of law in our contemporary American lives. The idea and practice of owning the wild, of owning nature, of taming the unpredictable, of managing the otherwise unmanaged is a Western framework of owning nature that is rooted in private property of primarily land, but can include air, water, even mineral rights (Steinberg 1995). In contrast to the Hawaiian system of land management of the *ahupua'a,* American practices of legalizing the spectacle through land management and property ownership may be less progressively grounded than they might otherwise seem as Pele will clean her house no matter what.

Illusions of containment

The performativity of law in protecting the spectacle results in the creation of the HVNP. Legal ownership over the volcano with controlled access renders the spectacle of Kīlauea a legal discourse in which the awe of the kinetic environment becomes the domain of law. Such legal positivism conveys the normative conceptualization of law at the volcano to be that of protection tethered to commodification. If legal positivism is the understanding that law's primacy is justified through its existence, law's attempted epistemological primacy of law over nature is typical of the Western approach of law to the environment in which the environment is subject to legal regulation. However, to attempt to control an environment that is dynamic and alive, as Kīlauea and similar landscapes are, is folly (Steinberg 1995) and a source of colonial conquest over the legal propertizing of wild terrain as manageable land (Spence 1999). As Sganga (2018, 11) notes "history shows that the idea, concept and legal institution of property are not set in stone, but rather subject to a constant diachronic evolution."

In Hawai'i, the performativity of law as having directive authority over the kinetic landscape is further tested by Hawaiian epistemologies that frame knowledge about the world *through* nature rather than *over* nature, even as nature includes and is a part of, rather than distinct from, humanity itself (Meyer 2003; Goodyear-Ka'ōpua et al. 2014). Such scholarship affirms that law's grip on the spectacle is fundamentally and essentially incomplete even while it continues to position itself as an authority over nature in a positivist light through safety regulations at the crater, criminalization of unauthorized access to active lava, even unsuccessful attempts to bomb advancing flows of lava to save the town of Hilo. Yet, land that is occupied by people is a form of nature that challenges Western legal frameworks of property as a commodity that is devoid of people in common legal understandings. This incomplete legal dominion over nature becomes especially apparent in law's response when confronting the capricious, actively dynamic landscape when the land itself changes when the volcano erupts beyond the constructed lines of the National Park. Unhindered by legal boundaries of the designated federal territory, lava unabashedly flows outside its jurisdictional parameters into private residential subdivisions and local communities and creates new terrain.

According to the Hawai'i Center for Volcanology at University of Hawai'i at Mānoa, the first written record of Kīlauea eruptions was in 1790. Prior to this, Hawaiian generational knowledge was passed down primarily orally to document eruptive events. As a revealing commentary on law's jurisdiction, the lava has consistently erupted beyond the boundaries of the National Park into areas of Hawai'i Island comprised of rural communities, small towns, and expansive private housing subdivisions. As one example, as noted by the United States Geological Survey (n.d.), in the 1955 Kalapana eruption, "lava flows destroyed 215 structures and buried 8.9 miles (14.3 km) of highway with lava as thick as 115 ft. (35m)." The depth of the lava was between 50–80 feet (15–25 m) of lava and covered 100 homes in the village of Kalapana. The village of Kalapana was buried as were numerous houses in the neighboring Royal Gardens subdivision. During this time, the lava flowed underground in lava tubes, over the ground in visible flows, and in and out of the boundaries of the HVNP. The fissure at Pu'u 'Ō'ō evolved through many stages: crater, cone, fissures, lava lake, collapsed cones, lava fountains, oozing streams of lava over the land emptying into the ocean. Beginning on January 3, 1983 and continuously for approximately thirty years, lava erupted from Kīlauea's East Rift Zone towards the ocean. In 2014, lava threatened the village of Pahoa and flowed within 400 yards of the town's commercial center (Cole and Nakaso 2018). In May 2018, a series of lava fissures erupted along the East Rift Zone. However, unlike the earlier Pāhoa lava flow four years prior, the Leilani Flow erupted in a residential neighborhood, the private subdivisions of Leilani Estates and Lanipuna Gardens. At the end of this eruption in August 2018, over twenty-four lava fissures opened covering 35.5 sq. km (13.7 miles) and adding 875 new acres of land to Hawai'i Island with the thickness of the lava/new land ranging from 55 to 280 m (180 to 919 ft.) (United States Geological Survey 2019). Fissure 8, the primary fissure in what had been Leilani Estates, spouted nearly 200 ft. in the air with an impressive display of fountaining molten lava.[3] Although there were few human injuries from molten lava, over 700 homes and countless other structures were inundated by the flowing lava.

In this context, property has multiple connotations. Whether as structures above ground, or the ground itself, American legal practices of property are based on idea of ownership and jurisdiction (Platt 2004; Purdy 2010; Linklater 2013). The kinetic epistemologies of nature as property foster a dynamic understanding of ownership insofar as property is actually a kinetic concept that may appear as static (real estate), as tangible (objects and things), or as conceptual (intellectual property). Property that is covered by a lava flow could change through the layering of new land, through burned buildings, through jurisdiction confusion over ownership of the new land. Ownership is also a kinetic concept insofar as private individuals, private groups, public groups, or public individuals may own property both formally but also informally, such as through squatter's rights. Jurisdiction is also a dynamic concept, as claim to place transpires through usage (Ford 2001; Brigham 2009). Kīlauea is an example of the fluidity of each of these concepts, property, ownership, and jurisdiction. Kīlauea is publicly owned through the U.S. government as a National Park, and through this public ownership, the public is allowed limited access. However, is access the same as ownership? Similarly ambiguous is lava as legal materiality as lava that has cooled may be owned through the building or acquisition of a lava rock wall, a common site for homes and businesses on Hawai'i Island. Active lava is often outside the jurisdiction of the National Park. Cooled lava, one form of which is cinder, is also a common material used in private landscaping or for the building and maintenance of public roads. Living with lava in its multiple forms is commonplace on volcanic islands such as the Big Island or Iceland. Yet, owning lava is much more complex despite its ubiquitous banality in Kīlauea's dynamically volcanic terrain.

Kinetic epistemologies of nature as property

Local celebrity and Puna resident Jack Thompson, once featured in Anthony Bourdain's *No Reservations*, once commented that "with lava, you can just step out of the way" (Paiva 2008). Thompson was the last resident of the Royal Gardens subdivision to have property inundated by multiple lava flows. When interviewed, Thompson noted that he felt much less threatened by lava than he did by earthquakes, forest fires, and other natural calamities. "Everything's fine up here in lava land," said Thompson. "I consider this a very safe place. We don't have a lot of the problems up here the rest of the world has" (Paiva 2008). Despite this nonchalance, as a homeowner, Thompson's property narrative was much less relaxed. I invited Thompson to speak to my university class about living with lava in Spring 2010. I was hoping he would describe the experience of living right next to an active lava; however, Thompson simply said that because he could outrun Pele, he was more concerned with the problems of local government. Having "gotten his mortgage down to zero,"[4] Thompson was angry at the local authorities because he had nothing to show for a house he had worked so hard to build and ultimately pay off. He was also troubled by the environmental impact assessments required of him to perform prior to his allowance of a friend's tourist helicopter land on his property. Because he had not done these assessments, the county inspectors had shut down the operation. As Thompson discovered, property ownership is somewhat of an illusion, particularly in this dynamic landscape.

When asked about the status of property ownership involving the 2018 Leilani eruption, Lisa Miura, Hawai'i County's real property tax administrator, stated: "The government does not claim ownership of all land covered by lava; the private property owner retains title even as the land's assessed value plummets to zero" (Donnelly 2018). In areas that have been inundated by lava, the value of property is assessed and taxed accordingly. For property that is assessed at $500 or less, the owner does not pay property tax. Miura's qualification of "all land" refers to the new land that is formed from lava flows that extends the shoreline. This coastal land extends the acreage of the state and is referred to as accretion. Accreted land is "new land created by a lava flow shall designate the 'State of Hawaii' as owner as established in the 1977 Hawai'i State Supreme Court case, *Kobayashi v. Zimring* and affirmed in the more recent Department of Land and Natural Resources, Amendment and Compilation of Chapter 13–222 Hawaii Administrative Rules from 2002."

It is through the layering of new land from lava that the island grows. Lava that has resulted in the jurisdictional extension of Hawai'i Island's land mass is legally referred to as accretion. Accreted lands become the property of the state as public domain land, as articulated in the precedent of *Kobayashi.* However, existing land that is covered and re-surveyed remains the property of the individual landowner. Lava that covers public land doesn't change the material aspects of the land and insofar as ownership is concerned, and that land is still in the public domain. Ownership of new land by the State of Hawai'i is reminiscent of the history of property ownership found in the Hawaiian *ahupua'a* in which communities owned the land as a group by living and working on the land and individual properties were not a part of the system. Yet, this contemporary concept of public ownership differs from the *ahupua'a* system insofar as land that is covered by lava is under competing jurisdictions within American law rather than belonging to just one community.

These competing jurisdictions range from federal to state to county to private forms of ownership and control over land. If lava covers land within the Park or extends the shoreline of the National Park, that land is owned by the U.S. (federal) government. In other words, if lava extends the shoreline outside the National Park and County of Hawai'i land, the land is owned by the State of Hawai'i. If land covers existing property, the land is devalued by the state for purposes of taxation and assessment, but still owned by the original property owner. Clearly, competing jurisdictional frameworks of property ownership are kinetic, just as the land itself is kinetic and constantly in flux. Legal historian Theodore Steinberg (1995, 5) keenly recognizes this and writes of the "folly of owning nature" in which "real estate is not as real, solid, or lasting as it may seem."

However, legal qualifications have been made concerning the capriciousness of Kīlauea's terrain in lower Puna. With massive land speculation of the lavafields of Hawai'i Island from the 1950s to the 1970s, numerous private housing subdivisions were created (Matsunami 1974; Nishida 1975; Cooper and Daws 1985). Among them was Leilani Estates, an area that fell squarely within Lava Zone 1. Lava Zone 1, located within the associated East Rift Zone, was a designation of the United States Geological Survey (USGS) in 1974 in the Lava Zone Map. Scientist for the USGS mapped areas where scientists determined the future flows of Kīlauea would most likely occur based upon historical lava activity. Yet, as the price of real estate was lower in these areas, many of the subdivisions created were located within or abutting Lava Zone 1. In fact, as many as 60% of the Big Island's speculative subdivision lots were located within the "USGS 'high risk' or 'highest risk' zones" (Cooper and Daws 1985, 264). Land was sold with the expectation that lava would flow again and that eruptive lava would "provide visitors with an opportunity to experience the awesome forces of nature" (Cooper and Daws 1985, 267). In the many years since, this forecast held true as visitors and residents within this volcanic zone did indeed have front row seats to lava in the front yards (Marusek 2012) as well as in their backyards as lava from Kīlauea has continuously covered countless houses, several villages, and roads since the 1950s.

In Puna, lava fields are open lots of land that real estate brokers sell and private property buyers purchase to develop. In asking the question, "How is it that some things get to be owned?," Steinberg (1995, 6 and 7) states: "property law is an expression of control over the natural world." In the case of nature that becomes property, control over nature an illusory attempt to manage the unmanageable. According to Cooper and Daws (1985, 259), land speculation resulting in the massive subdivisions of the Big Island was predicated on "sizeable acreage in remote areas, of little or no real economic use value, subdivided into house lots on which practically no one ever actually built homes." Echoing Thurston years later, the notion of *terra incognita* again came to justify owning nature through such property divisions. Yet, we know that what was viewed as empty lava fields without use was actually vital land historically inhabited by Hawaiians for generations prior with much different practices of land ownership. One such example aside from the ahupua'a is in the Ka'ū desert district downslope from Halema'uma'u Crater known as Keonehelelei (the Footprints region). Here, open and lava/ash-covered land, seen as empty by the outside viewer similar to the land speculators of the Puna lava fields, was a well-known route for travel as well as repository for volcanic glass used for toolmaking, woodworking, and weaponry (Moniz Nakamura 2003). Therefore, the narrative of *terra incognita*, while evoking a shift in the socio-legal qualities of property that is relevant to the larger history of Hawai'i and Hawai'i island, is still seen as unchanged through the claim of nature as property whether through public national park lands or in land speculation in Puna resulting in private subdivisions.

Yet, the quality of hardened lava is solid rock. This material solidification of the landscape that characterizes the lavascape of Hawai'i Island yields an illusion of stability. As unstable land at the ocean's edge that looks on the surface to be solid rock, lava shelves and lava deltas, or new land from hardened lava, can actually cracks, collapses, and falls into the ocean. Lava shelves can happen as lava flowing onto itself basically builds a shelf without a solid foundation to support it from underneath. As the weight of the shelf increases and is barraged by the wave action of the sea crashing against the new land, the seemingly stable land can fall into the ocean often without much warning in a geological phenomenon known as lava shelf collapse.

In the lavascape, the infrastructure of the natural environment involves the natural architecture that spatially constructs the landscape. Such natural architecture is rooted in the ground as it moves. Likewise, those people who inhabit the surface are also moving and shape the perceived stability within the lavascape. For example, the populated landscape of Lava Zone One involves land that appears stable but is actually the crust over active lava. Or, at Halema'uma'u Crater within the National Park are places were both land and people are in motion. In managing this lavascape, conservation and nature are legally imbued frameworks of regulation that define place and its occupancy (Hale 2016).

Yet, it's not only the land that is unstable but also the law itself. Law is never fully stable, as it is a phenomenon interpreted through the dynamism of culture that itself evolves over time. Like the fluidity of lava above and below the surface of the earth, law is constantly in flux. Constituted through culture(s), law is never neutral, never static, and is generally unpredictable despite its appearance of a solid foundation of courts and legislation. In this way, the lavascape is similar to the lawscape insofar as the vista of accessibility to knowledge, power, and even jurisdictional frameworks are fluid and kinetic in their conceptual understandings and practices. Furthermore, the lavascape at Kīlauea illustrates that law itself is a form of accretion in which the additions in the lawscape of what law is grow the body of law as claimed through public knowledge of legality. Law is as kinetic as the lavaflow of Kīlauea, sometimes slow and oozing, but other times fast and seemingly out of control.

Accretion of law in the lavascape

The lavascape is a legal landscape of layering, whether as layers of jurisdiction, as newly accreted land or in designations of land ownership. The lavascape is also a layering of hazard and risk that upon first glance seems calm, even safe as the twentieth century Americans framed it. Hazards are possibly immediate, as new land is often unstable and can break off unexpectedly. Or, it's still too hot. Some roads have been repaved even as the asphalt is soft from the heat coming from the earth (Salmons 2019). Yet, the hazards are also layered through cartographic representations (such as the Lava Zone Map), visual designations of property ownership (County Tax Map Key (TMK) maps or Subdivision maps), and even cracks in roads from the molten energy underneath (as happened in several places during the eruptive summer of 2018). The stability of land at Kīlauea is an illusion because the land itself is unstable. As a result, the law that governs this instability is also constantly in motion with energy released in spurts like the periodic eruptions of the volcano. The kineticism of law includes the formalities of park rangers and local law enforcement to the cultural realities of children who choose to write earnest letters to Pele on red pieces of paper taped to their school fence during the Pahoa eruption (La Ganga 2014) rather than to the Director of the Civil Defense Agency for help. Culturally, with Pele in charge, the normativity of law over nature is incomplete, particularly as the flowing lava ultimately did stop before reaching the school grounds. In this way, faith in the Western approach to law as the ultimate keeper of the environment confronts indigenous epistemological frameworks that preceded

Americanized legal dominance of the twentieth century and endures into the present day.

In this way, the relationship between law and nature seeks to ensconce those on the landscape while ensuring the environment is under control. The politics of hazard in the populated landscape reveal law's response to the active lavascape with layers of accretion resulting from law's response to nature's dynamic forces. In law's attempt to tame the prowess of active lava, law itself extends its reaches through military presence, enhanced frameworks of criminality, and jurisdictional response within the social order. The materiality of fluid lava results in the illusory performativity of law as an authority over the moving terrain as a frontier of governance.

As contemporary conquest of law's jurisdiction through land ownership, the private ownership of the spectacle becomes contested terrain as calls for the state to assume ownership of the new land at Leilani have surfaces (Lauer 2018). However, ownership is private only up to a point, as private property remains as private property, with the possible exception of the landowner of where Fissure 8 erupted. Fissure 8 was the largest fissure. It marks the Leilani eruption in its height and public character. Although Leilani Estates is still a privately owned residential neighborhood, flocks of visitors come by car to the neighborhood to witness the spectacle of the 2018 eruption. Despite the complaints of increased public presence in the neighborhood, the area remains public, as the neighborhood is neither gated nor off limits to non-residents. The neighborhood streets are public. Fissure 8 is now a public spectacle even though it sits on what was private property. The visibility of ownership through land markers is particularly compelling as houses are above ground and any property markers (and houses) are buried and now seem as *terra incognita* in terms of property ownership. While the County of Hawai'i Real Property Division values such land with $0 taxes, the ownership over the lava-covered land is disputed. *Kobayashi* only addresses the ownership of accreted land that extended the shoreline. However, landowners still own their land and can have it re-surveyed to show the boundaries despite the covering of lava. Many landowners rebuild over the lava using off-grid utilities. However, again, jurisdictional frameworks come into play as land that is covered by lava within the National Park remains the property of the federal government. And for those private landowners who do rebuild, chances are quite good that because the lava inundated land is valued by the County at $0, paying or collecting property for legality's sake is likely not a strong priority or concern for law in general. Furthermore, as most people who rebuild build unpermitted structures (permits according to local construction guidelines) and do not have their property surveyed because the County does not require this, it can sometimes happen where houses that have been built are actually built on someone else's land.

Even as the landscape of Kīlauea evolves, so too does law within the lavascape. If we return to hazard, we can see that law seeks to right itself through its own creation. Think about the following example. On December 31, 2016, five onlookers, who had crossed under the hazard ropes at the lava viewing area, were followed by a ranger. This ranger convinced them finally to return to the designated safe area. Fifteen minutes later, the lava shelf collapsed into the ocean (Hawai'i Emergency Management Agency 2017). Because of where the ropes were, individual reckoning of common sense was faulty in superseding legal rationale that, with scientific backing, sought to protect onlookers from collapsing land where the lava meets the sea. The idea of sneaking under the rope is a consistent tension that exists at the volcano, and at the geyser. The view of the role of man and the role of the law in protecting people is evocative of a larger tension involving individual common sense and compliance with external laws (with the image of a rope that safely should not be crossed as one example). At the geyser, there was a short, small, seemingly benign rope that represented the law (or some unknown entity that was "in the know"). Crossing the rope meant literally treading on boiling ground, as the steam and bubbles could be viewed from the other side. However, what happens when the other side isn't visible. Curiosity takes over and individual determinations of common sense take over for law, as law (in the form of a rope) can be easily crossed. The justification of this crossing is that law is not really in the know, and that the individual knows better. Of course, there are risks; yet, there are also risks inherent to the positioning of the rope by law, namely that this localized site of danger will remain within the confines of the rope. However, maybe law doesn't care, and only cares to protect itself. This was the case in the lava shelf collapse, when the ropes were moved back and the idea was generated that the ropes are the keys to safety – for as previously stated, law knows best.

To conclude, the constant flow of an active volcano results in the production of spectacle. Law seeks to manage this spectacle either through national parks or emergency frameworks by determining risk and hazard in accordance with predictability. While the natural spectacle is fluid in its eruption, either as lava, or molten rock, or the superheated water of a geyser, legal responses to spectacle are themselves fluid types of law that evolve as spectacles transpire. The spectacle of landscape change is a natural phenomenon, but a legal one as well as implicating jurisdictional and cultural fluctuations. Creating legal boundaries around such places is an attempt by law to contain and preserve this land as public. Yet, the idea of public is itself limiting, particularly when compared to indigenous forms of land ownership. Through the making public of these places, the government is rendered in charge as master determinant of risk and access. We can see this, as national parks become methods of land management that normalize hazards associated with volcanic and geothermal spectacle. Interestingly, the framing of risk is one that assumes a legal positioning akin to paternalism in which the state assumes and performs legality as framed through the knowledge of risk.

Notes

1 The use of the Hawaiian *ʻokina* and other punctuation would not have been used by Ford in 1911, so the quote appears here as it would have in 1911.
2 As the use of Hawaiian diacriticals is a contemporary practice in academic literature, I have left the early-twentieth century American writings involving Hawaiʻi as they would have appeared (such as Hawaii).
3 At the time of writing, Fissure 8 is undergoing a name change to give the new land a Hawaiian name.
4 In Spring 2010, I invited Thompson to speak to my university class about living with lava. Instead, he offered a property narrative as he spoke about his relationship with local government concerning his piece of land in Royal Gardens. This quote is taken from the notes I recorded during his talk.

Chapter 3

Legalizing the spectacle

Tourism is the experience of seeing, witnessing, and being at the spectacle. Tourism to a spectacle often involves the absence of local knowledge, but not always. Often, tourists can be local residents visiting the spectacle. While at the spectacle, the visiting public is protected by those who govern the spectacle. Yet, the protection is incomplete, as the touristic assumption of risk by the visiting public necessarily predicates the experience of visiting the spectacle, particularly in kinetic environments. Visitors' common sense also comes into play in assuming the role of tourist, but even common sense depends upon the various knowledge of the legal backdrop of the spectacle. For example, the culture of law and legal protectionism may be different in Iceland than it is in Hawai'i. And even within each place, these perspectives may differ. These differences engage an enlivened sense of law in which the constitutive give and take between place and culture, risk and common sense is fluid and constantly evolving.

In Hawai'i at Kīlauea, lava is a force that challenges the legal positivist presumption that law is responsible in guarding the visitor from risk. Furthermore, lava, through a variety of venues, reveals the performative quality of law in which the spectacle seems to be under the control of law. Whether as official sanctioned viewpoints of molten lava, special permits for media to go beyond the protective ropes even as the public is restricted, or even as elected officials themselves visit the spectacle on behalf of the restricted public, moving lava characterizes the kinetic environment as a spectacle in which the visibility of law counters the visibility of the spectacle. This chapter examines the performativity of law in terms of access and regulation to eruption inside the Hawai'i Volcanoes National Park (HVNP) as well as outside the national park in lava-viewing areas set up by the County of Hawai'i Civil Defense Agency.

Legal performativity in kinetic environments

Molten lava is an enticing, dramatic, and rare visual spectacle that is a recurrent aspect of living on Hawai'i Island. Hawai'i Island, also called the Big Island of Hawai'i, is home to five volcanoes. Of these, Kīlauea, located within the HVNP, has been actively producing lava since 1983. The most recent event began on May 4, 2018, when following a 6.9 magnitude earthquake, 26 fissures began to open in a residential subdivision. At the most active fissure, Fissure 8,[1] lava fountained nearly 200 ft. into the air. Contributing to the eruption's legal complexity, the majority of these fissures erupted within two residential subdivisions, the larger Leilani Estates and the smaller neighboring subdivision of Lanipuna Gardens. Yet, this was not an unusual occurrence, as lava erupting from Kīlauea has inundated inhabited areas of East Hawai'i Island since 1750, a date recorded by the Hawai'i Center for Volcanology (Rubin, n.d.). Previous to this Leilani flow, lava had come within a mile of inundating the village of Pāhoa in 2014. Although Pāhoa residents had been largely spared from any lava-related damage, when the Leilani eruption ended late in the summer of 2018, over 700 homes had been destroyed by flowing lava (Fujimori 2018).

From her home deep within Halema'uma'u Crater at Kīlauea's summit caldera, Madame Pele, the Hawaiian Goddess of Fire, resides within the contemporary parameters of the HVNP. With her glow of lava often visible from deep within the crater, Kīlauea has many *Pu'u*, or vents, that open up as she travels to the ocean. From a legal perspective, the lava often flows outside the jurisdictional boundaries of the national park, as this spectacle of molten lava cannot be restricted to the boundaries imposed upon it by the mapped territory of the national park and the federal government. Instead, Madame Pele exercises her right of way to flow wherever she would like and lava indiscriminately crosses private property and public land. This resulting *lavascape* is the socio-legal landscape of the volcanic spectacle that temporally transpires from molten lava to cooled earth while complicating jurisdictional understandings and practices (Ford 2001). Lavascape is this sense is therefore similar to the lawscape of Philippopoulos-Mihalopoulos (2018, 5), who describes responsibility as "typically a juridical term" and as "one of the main lawscape mechanisms for negotiating law and space." For those seeking to seek the glow of Kīlauea, the law and space of an active volcano, or lavascape, stands to juxtapose the jurisdictional prerogative of restricting access to seeing the glow against the visual desires of thrill-seeking tourists.

The experience of seeing the glow of molten lava is a spectacle that is rare, captivating, and either a source of pleasure (if sightseeing), of sacred awe (through religious reverence) or of apprehension (if faced with lava inundation and the loss of property and/or access from erupting lava). At Kīlauea, such a spectacle legally transpires according to the place where the lava either glows or flows. For visitors to the HVNP, lava has glowed peacefully within the natural confines of Halema'uma'u Crater. In the 1950s, fountaining lava could be viewed at close proximity at Kīlauea Iki. Most recently, lava within the Crater at the volcano's summit caldera most recently from 2008 until 2018. The fiery, yet quiet orange glow was best visible at nighttime from the viewing overlook at Jaggar Museum at the edge of the caldera. Here, the lava lake within the crater was at optimal viewing distance, with the glow visible through the cloud of volcanic emissions rising into the sky. The ability to literally see the color of molten earth became a primary attraction for park visitors, with over two million visitors witnessing the lava's glow prior to its disappearance in May 2018 (Hawai'i Volcanoes National Park, n.d. (a)). Legally, this glow was under the federal jurisdiction of the U.S. Department of the Interior, who controlled entry to the caldera, created the park's boundaries, and patrolled its visitation. In response to the changes resulting from the Leilani flow while concurrently recognizing the attraction of the glow for those visiting the park, the park's website alerts visitors that "There is no molten lava or lava glow to see anywhere in or out of the park" (Hawai'i Volcanoes National Park, n.d.(b)). Prior to the Leilani eruption, seeing the glow of lava was a rare and legally framed spectacle within the park's jurisdiction. Yet, this jurisdictional framework is much more complex than just the federal-izing of the volcano might appear.

Prior to the 2018 Leilani eruption, when the lava flowed outside the national park's boundaries as it did at Pu'u 'Ō'ō on Kīlauea's southern flank, the lava glow could be publicly viewed at a distance through the periodic installation of localized lava-viewing areas set up by the County of Hawai'i's Civil Defense Agency, a locally responsive extension of the Federal Emergency Management Agency that is organically responsive to the needs of County of Hawai'i. It is the "role of the Civil Defense Agency is to direct and coordinate the development and administration of the County's total emergency preparedness and response program to ensure prompt and effective action when natural or man-caused disaster threatens or occurs anywhere in the County of Hawai'i" (Hawai'i County Civil Defense n.d.). Threat to the County ranges from tsunami, nuclear threat, earthquake, hurricane, volcanoes, to manmade disasters. As stated, volcanic activity falls under local jurisdiction as natural disaster.

Lava-viewing areas of the Civil Defense were created in order to harness the flow of people and cars who traveled to see the glow at night wherever it could be found. These lava-viewing areas were managed in a way similar to the Crater Overlook within the national park, with ranger-like Civil Defense enforcement personnel stationed to patrol the activities of the sightseeing public. Yet here, gates and boundaries at the impromptu lava-viewing areas were much less restrictive and much more porous than at the national park, with visitors able to venture beyond the guard shacks once the guards left in the evenings usually around ten o'clock. Because the staffing of these guard shacks was financially limited and did not extend to twenty-four hours a day, risk was assumed to be in the hands of the visitor rather than of the county, state, and/or federal government. Interestingly, it is this assumption of risk that attracts visitation to the spectacle and serves as the source of law's tension with the kinetic environment in a phenomenologically positioning of law's primacy over nature.

By tethering the framework of risk to assertions of jurisdiction over nature, the legal spectacle of Kīlauea's glow is primarily regulated through viewing access. Despite the official sanctioning of lava-viewing areas whether in the national park or by the Civil Defense Agency, the glow itself is enticing enough to compel many people to stray beyond law's boundaries, rangers, and guard shacks to experience it on their own despite the risk of individual harm. In this way, sightseeing is an activity that has the power to threaten the stability of law. In a society of law and order, it might be presumed that chaos will ensue if jurisdiction is not enforced and the visual imagination not legally regulated. Yet, the visual spectacle of the lavascape as it is harnessed through a legalized imagination that exists through jurisdictional boundaries, images of enforcements, and topological mappings of where the lava has flowed and will likely flow next creates an understanding of individual risk that is attractive rather than repellant. Rather than control the sightseer, chaos can be found instead in law's choice to frame nature as property subject to the layers of jurisdiction.

Molten lava glows. Especially at night. On clear nights, the quiet orange glow at the Kīlauea Caldera from deep within Halema'uma'u Crater contrasted the brightness of the Milky Way from the overlook at Jaggar Museum in the HVNP. On cloudy nights, the glow was visibly accentuated against the foggy backdrop of misty haze. Sometimes, the stillness of this spectacle was broken by the rumbling of boulders from the crater's sides tumbling into the churning lake of lava. Since the eruption of March 19, 2008, the crater had just been getting larger, as the vent inside the crater had increased significantly in diameter. The level of the lava lake inside the vent rose and fell as the lava inflated and deflated. When the lava was high enough, the glow became more visible. In May 2015 at a peak in recent lava inflation, the lava actually overflowed the crater's edges. A rare sight to behold, the glow drew a record number of visitors to the park. During this time, viewing the glow meant waiting in traffic for several hours on the Chain of Craters Road that bordered the summit within the park.[2] On May 11, 2018, the park closed due to ash eruptions at the summit, which followed and subsequently coincided with the opening of lava fissures in the lower Puna subdivision, Leilani Estates. The actual seeing of the glow from molten lava is framed as a legal spectacle in terms of the stability of law that is threatened through unregulated sightseeing. In the past, regulated access to the eruptive activity of Kīlauea was much more relaxed, as Figures 3.1 and 3.2 indicate. The proximity of the viewing public to eruptive activity was much less at a distance than it is today, depicted from behind a wall a mile from the crater in Figure 3.3.

Since the 1950s however, new hazards frame the discourse of the national park and its relationship with the public, whether local or visiting.

> Residents of the island of Hawai'i....face the unique hazards that go along with living on the slopes of an active volcano. These hazards

Figure 3.1 Spectators view another explosion cloud from the Volcano House Hotel at Kīlauea Volcano (May 24, 1924). Available at: https://volcanoes.usgs.gov/volcanoes/kilauea/geo_hist_1924_halemaumau.html

Figure 3.2 Kīlauea Iki Volcano erupting, Big Island of Hawaii (1955). Available at: https://commons.wikimedia.org/wiki/Category:Kīlauea_Iki#/media/File:Kilauea_Iki_erupting_1959.JPG

Figure 3.3 Visitors observe the summit eruption of Kīlauea from the safe vantage point at the observation deck at Jaggar Museum, one-mile away from Halema'uma'u Crater (2017). Available at: https://www.nps.gov/havo/learn/news/030817guide.htm.

> include lava flows, volcanic gases, and earthquakes. The long-term, most recent eruption of Kīlauea started January 3, 1983 [and ending with the Leilani events of 2018] has destroyed more than 180 houses and buried 8 miles of highway and utility lines. To help prevent loss of life and property from eruptions and earthquakes, USGS scientists are working to increase our ability to predict these natural events and to education the public about the hazards in their area (U.S. Department of the Interior and U.S. Geological Survey n.d.).

Now, the active presence and future threat of lava presents real danger rather than just a harmless spectacle. This real danger and its prediction are the basis now for governance. Public education of these hazards and the restriction of visitors is now not as much of a free for all as it seemed to have been when the HVNP was first formed. Take for instance the element of distance to the spectacle. Before, visitors could walk right up to the edge of the Halamaumau caldera, which at that time was a lake of boiling lava. Now, the Jaggar Museum and site of the Hawaiian Volcano Observatory (maintained by the USGS) are positioned on the rim of the same larger caldera; however now, the molten lava at the summit is not accessible to the public but is restricted to scientists. Additionally, the Chain of Craters Road is now blocked from public access due to volcanic fumes.

In static environments where the earth itself does not move, the legal regulation of spectacle is site-specific and routinely occurs on land that is stable, i.e. the sidewalk (Blomley 2011), the street (Kohn 2004), the zoo (Braverman 2013), and the shopping mall (Dovey 1999) despite the movement that occurs. In the sense that the ground is stable means that it does not move. In contrast, the land at Kīlauea Volcano is moving as felt through routine earthquakes or seen at Halema'uma'u. Distance between the visiting public and the spectacle is the regulation of access to the spectacle in the name of safety from eruptive events. As the lava churns, the spectacle of seeing molten rock move is a spectacle of fluidity insofar as the solidity of rock is destabilized through its heated liquidity. Buttressed against law's regulation of the moving landscape, law governs this instability by overseeing access to its movement. In other words, the glow itself is not regulated and cannot be regulated by law, but access to the glow can be. Is lava beyond legal regulation? That would depend on its propensity to be regulated or governed. In this way, access to see the glow engenders the lavascape, or law's attempt to regulate the spectacle of the molten lava. The legal metaphor of watching nature is both voyeuristic, but also observational and tamed as the glow becomes an abstracted visual of a landscape that seems fixed but is really just resting within the confines of the crater *at the moment.*

By either private vehicle or tourist bus, visitors come from all over the world to experience this spectacle, and cars fill the museum's parking lot at all hours but particularly at night. From the perspective of a visiting public, the kinetic environment at Halema'uma'u Crater is a spectacle to watch and to experience. Viewing the glow from molten lava is the visual witnessing of raw earth. The vibrant orange radiating from the earth seems more ethereal than earthly. Yet, in the national park, the glow is harnessed by the legal framing of its viewability. This glow of dynamic earth that boils within the crater and is visible from the caldera's rim at the overlook provides a keen juxtaposition between the stability of the national park in containing the spectacle and the instability of molten lava and its eruptive potential. Similar to a caged animal at a zoo, lava seems to be "kept" within the confines of the park's boundaries with the overlook as viewing platform. The overlook, with its knee-high walls of cooled lava rock and museum displayed that provide a narrative of conquered wilderness, is similar to seeing a tiger or lion at a safe distance while at the zoo. In the Museum, a variety of lava rocks were on display as well as the outfit of a scientist who had the misfortune to stand on instable lava. Yet, through this constructed setting in which an active seismograph was paradoxically positioned adjacent a gift shop and faced a large painting of Madame Pele, the Hawaiian Goddess of Fire, who resides at Kīlauea. Here, the threat of danger seemed lessened just as tigers and polar bears seem benign, if not content within a zoo setting. Until the unexpected closure of the national park in response to the nearly daily eruptions and earthquakes at the summit in early May 2018, lava was viewable from a safe distance at the overlook. Lava that is alive, with the potential to grow, expand, and even erupt beyond its crater confines (as it had during the overflow in May 2015), is contained by the legal framing of the national park and with Madame Pele encapsulated within the contemporary American boundaries of materializing nature.

Or, so we see it as such. As visitors to the park, we see the lava in the crater as dangerous and wild, yet seemingly unchanging at a safe distance. We feel the possibility of eruption, the nearness of the magma within our vantage point. We witness the rawness of the glowing magma and defer to the tranquility of the scene. Through the park's framing of this view, we view the glow as law would want us to, through the legal consciousness that defers to law's ostensible control over this place. Similar to Ewick and Silbey's (1998) triadic analysis of law's operationalization through legal consciousness, visitors at the overlook conflate law with lava insofar as law (and lava as law's forced accomplice) expects deference to restrictions on viewing (*before* the law), engagement in the form of enjoy the access to view the glow (*with* the law), and sometimes (to be explored later in the chapter) resistance to staying behind the overlook's lavarock walls (*against* the law). Yet, law at the overlook is dependent upon an Americanized expectation of law to govern (Tyler 2006; Levinson 1998). Ironically, the overlook conveys the idea that law already knows what the limits of the danger inherent to the spectacle are. As visitors, we assume that law has our best interests in mind; conversely, law expects that we defer to legal structures of regulation in this environment. As Scott (1998) describes, law is a force that can quell the unknown chaos of nature in ways that challenge common sense and reframe assertions of normativity. In this way, law's management of the wild, whether through forest design or constructing accessibility to a volcano's glow, is a paradox involving a tension of land ownership, environmental preservation, and historical nationalist conquest.

Seeing lava and the glow that it produces against the night sky reminds us of the power that nature has and how small and expendable we really are in comparison. Seeing the peaceful orange glow from this lava, contained deep within Halema'uma'u Crater, masks the reality of molten earth bubbling and churning existing just a short distance away. Lava that does not seem to present any danger by appearing as distantly peaceful glow seems to convey a sense of power of human over nature. The juxtaposition of public safety against potential threat supports the legal framing of viewing active nature from the setting of a national park. Arguably, active lava can kill. Yet, despite the threatened danger, the glow remains a spectacle of wildness that law seeks to harness by controlling access to its viewing. At the overlook, law serves as gatekeeper to the spectacle. The controlled experience of viewing this natural phenomenon is the metamorphosis of law from a position of observer to an agent of control in this untamed place where the earth bubbles on its own time and in its own way. Law at the park provides the access for viewing and surrounds this hole in the earth's crust through its constructed boundaries. These boundaries, whether at the park's gate, the road to the Jaggar Museum, or at the overlook on the crater's rim, frame the glow as a legal spectacle. As such, law claims jurisdiction over this dynamic landscape. Yet while we know that lava itself cannot be owned, the land around the vent is less independent (i.e. mobile), has less agency, and succumbs to a form of governance exercised by Madame Pele.

Law serves as host at Halema'uma'u to millions of visitors from around the world who visit the park each year.[3] The experience of seeing the lava's glow provides visitors with a touristic currency, which in turn, has historically driven (and to some, justified) law's dominance in this environment through the existence of the park. If tourism is experience-gaining by a leisure class (MacCannell 2013), then seeing the glow becomes the currency of a tourist class that can be spent as cultural and social capital. The social capital that comes from seeing actual lava that is molten and contained in the crater is an experience to tell others about. The park provides a venue for obtaining this capital. Historically, the spectacle became legalized through the creation of park. In a colonizing fashion, the park opened up Kīlauea to global tourism under the auspices of a American jurisdiction over this kinetic landscape. Previous to the park, Halema'uma'u and Kīlauea more generally, was a previously untamed and sacred place (sacred to the Hawaiians who worshipped Pele). Today, the park manages the lavascape through the Museum's overlook structure (with rock wall, signs, binocular viewing stations), controlling access to the glow (driving on the crater's rim through the park to the parking lot at the museum, maintaining a lack of lighting in order to allow visitors to fully experience glowing lava at night, hiring park officials who manage traffic in the parking lot), as well as providing for visitors' safety at the glow (distance between the overlook and the active vent, providing rangers who chase people who go beyond the ropes, even portraying the presence of a ranger afterhours as a cardboard silhouette of a ranger peering out from the windows of the museum).

The idea of containment as related to access to the spectacle is particularly evident in the physical architecture of the overlook. Standing behind the walls at the overlook frames the lavascape through a managed boundary. In the window of the museum, the silouetted cut-out of a ranger was positioned to convey ongoing surveillance once the museum closed in the evening indicating that law is present and ready to govern through the panopticonic gaze of the everwatchful presence of the park ranger. Yet, more often than not, rangers were constantly present. One evening in 2015, I visited Halema'uma'u at night during a period of inflation, when the glow from the lava is very visible. As I came out of the lighted museum into the darkened overlook full of people, I witnessed two agitated park rangers discussing something seemingly urgent. One of them climbed over the lava rock wall barrier towards the crater's edge. This barrier is about 2-ft. high and made out of lava rock. Although the ranger wore a jacket with reflecting tape and help only a small flashlight, the ranger disappeared into the night intent on apprehending an errant visitor who had crossed over the wall. Crossing the rock wall and traversing along the crater's edge at night was a particular hazard during the daytime, but at night, even more so. From the perspective of law, crossing the wall was not only an error in common sense, but an invitation for the subsequent discipline of attendant rangers. Through the silhouetted form, law's presence is personified even when rangers aren't physically present to run after visitors on the loose.

Through the boundary and the distancing provided by the overlook, the spectacle seemed under control. This distance and subsequent control of law over the potentially chaotic generates the lavascape as legal metaphor of chaos under control. Law has similar boundaries, visible as the police officer's uniform, the judge's black gown, or the formal austerity inherent to the courthouse. Law is seemingly inaccessible in these examples with the potential disruption kept at a distance. Yet, just as regular folks can pose as police officers, we might question law's stability. How stable really is law when we ignore it, such as when we cross over the overlook's walls or defy a ranger's instructions? Isn't law really then rather similar to a molten crater of lava? Bubbling and churning, visible, yet distant, law that is perceived as creating distance is law that is under threat from a less distanced approach to governing found in individual common sense. As seen at the overlook, law attempts to manage, but is challenged by visitors' individualized interpretations of danger, risk, threat that challenge its ultimate authority at the crater's rim. Therefore, the distanced glow of molten lava managed by park rangers as well as by individual common sense serves as a metaphor for law that is similar to seeing the glow as peaceful and calm from a distance, but contained and managed by (in)accessibility and distance through legal formalism. National parks are governmental sites that preserve a natural setting for public enjoyment. In this sense, public enjoyment translates to the ability (if not right) to visit the area and to view a natural setting with protection by government in terms of access accompanied by a translated understanding of the particular phenomenon. The framing of these places is often built around special natural landscapes framed as legal spectacles. This protection is set up also for visitors' sake, as the natural phenomenon within park boundaries is often wild and on the move. Whether active lava or exploding water from a geyser, the act of prediction contributes to the epistemological foundations for regulation, as active volcanoes are scientifically studied and monitored and some geysers erupt in a timely fashion. The relationship of nature to law as premised upon flow of land and people contributes to a unique understanding of legal regulation and jurisdiction in such environments. As the attempt to manage risk and preserve nature, national parks seem to provide law with a tangible grip of control over the kinetic terrain, as predictability tethered to visitation serves as the foundation, if not justification, for such regulation.

More or less public?

As we've seen, such natural phenomena are not limited to occurring on public land and often happen on privately owned property sites. The complexity of land and its relationship to law as publicly usable and/or privately owned challenges normative conceptualizations about property ownership and are engendered through law and called into question as lava cools, hardens, and creates new land. The glow of lava can also be seen outside the boundaries of the HVNP as it the flow of molten lava trickles over the landscape and down the pali (cliffs) of Kīlauea's southern flank towards the ocean. The viewing of active flows coming from Pu'u 'Ō'ō Vent in the Puna District of Hawai'i Island is regulated by the Hawai'i County Civil Defense Agency. Civil Defense regularly sets up lava-viewing areas for the public to see the glow at night whenever the lava is visible to the naked eye. These sites, bustling with tourists and local commercialism, reveal the fluidity of law in its ongoing regulation of lava that challenges the normativity of law's authoritative presence. Sandy Kedar (2014) speaks about the importance of "studying legalities as embedded in social, cultural, and especially *spatial* {sic} settings." In Hawai'i, legality involving land is embedded in the 'aina, or Hawaiian relationship between land and people. Under the ali'i, or Hawaiian royalty, there was not individualized ownership of land, but instead a communal division of the land into districts that reached from mauka (the mountains) to makai (the sea), known as the ahupua'a system. Once the U.S. Government overthrew Queen Lili'uokalani of the Kingdom of Hawai'i in 1893, the Crown Lands previously controlled by the Kingdom were ceded to the American government and placed in the public domain.

Epistemologically, land in Hawai'i, specifically at Halema'uma'u, is a lawscape epitomizing the Western colonization of the native and of nature. Not only was land taken, but the Western framework of ownership also overtook the land and the spectacle. No longer was Kīlauea an agent of its own (as Pele worshipped in her home environment of Kīlauea), but rather a wild place to be governed within the jurisdiction of the HVNP. This Americanized view of the spectacle is an extension of law's positioning in order to control nature and civilize the native in the kinetic lawscape. This reserve is rooted in the preservation of the natural, yet changing environment. Regulations associated with the evolving spectacles reveals a larger statement about how law works, namely as an overarching, better knowing entity that seeks to protect, yet also maintain control over that which is framed as hazard. This isn't to suggest that the changing natural environment is free from hazards, but instead to examine the idea of hazard from the position of a perspectivized authority that frames and interprets that hazard absence, in large part as separate from individualized common sense notions of hazard and danger. What results are conflicting notions of authority that are rooted in differing societal values found in property

(American versus Icelandic) that create or can be reframed as dependency upon law to access the natural spectacle. Property over lava that has cooled will be examined in subsequent chapters throughout the book. This dependency upon law spins off into other areas in which law is seen as a paternalistic guide, a source of knowledge that often goes unquestioned for its legitimacy. Indigeneity stands also to challenge western law's authority to determine common sense, as western law, at least in Hawaii, is a new-ish phenomenon.

Similar to the visibility of lava at Halema'uma'u Crater, witnessing the glow of lava is a compelling tourist attraction. In contrast to the Crater though, the lava at Pu'u 'Ō'ō is on the move. This movement is the enlivenment of earth as it travels over the landscape from the vent to the ocean. Lava is on the move. And, just as lava travels across the land, so are people who want to watch it move. As it creeps over the landscape, the glow from flowing lava lights up the night sky and draws visitors from land and by sea. As Kīlauea's lava as it moves out of the national park and into neighboring residential communities, law's jurisdiction is fluid. "Legal places may literally move in space" as "moving legal places are often a result of moving people" as Franz and Keebet von Benda-Beckmann (2014, 31) describe. Yet despite this tenuous framework, the active flow of lava erupting from Kīlauea's southestern flank at Pu'u 'Ō'ō volcanic cone has resulted in impromptu lava-viewing areas set up for public viewing of the flow by the Hawai'i County Civil Defense Agency. Additionally, the U.S. Coast Guard maintains a presence at the lava's ocean entry managing the proximity of privately run lava boat tours. As a project in legal legibility (Scott 1998), the United States Geological Survey (USGS) has formulated a Lava Zone Map recording past flows and predicting directions of future flows. These initiatives are buttressed by law's local response to the recent June 27, 2014, Lava Flow in the lower Puna District of Hawai'i Island.

Yet, indigenous Hawaiian ways of knowing and dealing with volcanic activity may epistemologically challenge the need for present-day law to control, regulate, and constrain an active lava flow and its access. Additionally, the actions by a few individuals who seek to "play" with nature may contradict normative paradigms of risk associated with molten lava (and superheated water in Iceland). Nonetheless, related to law's project of colonization discussed in chapter one, the prediction of hazard and the management of risk coalesce to characterize law's presence in this instable terrain. As legal turf, we know that law governs not only through command, but also through responses to the resistance of its legal ordering and territoriality (Delaney 2010). Outside the clearly defined boundaries of the HVNP, localized cultural and social resistance to law's governability of nature provides the opportunity for law to reassert itself in novel ways as assumable gatekeeper for the kinetic environment. As "folk geographies" (Benda-Beckmann 2014) or "folk legalities" (Marusek 2014), these localized understandings of living in spaces on the slopes of an active volcano generate "multiple legal constructions of space [that] open up diverse arenas for the exercise of political authority and the localization of rights and obligations".[4] On Hawai'i Island, indigenous knowledge informs local practice and sometimes conflicts, sometimes compliments a westernized practice of American law in this place of Pele. And for those who want to witness or monitor from afar, the webcams operated by the USGS and the Hawaiian Volcano Observatory are available online and allows the public to watch the bubbling through a technological, ever watchful and recording eye. Law depends upon geological authorities (science) as non-law-based actors to provide legal information. For example, at the site of the lava flow going into the ocean, law works with scientists to warn the public of dangers. Similarly, through this vantage point, the level of the lava becomes apparent through measurement which assists with the interpretation seeing the less obvious when directly looking at the crater.

In lower Puna on Hawai'i Island, the Hawai'i County Civil Defense has set up lava-viewing areas, as seen in Figure 3.4. These areas are monitored by local officials and are open to the public. These places are intended to

Figure 3.4 Lava-viewing areas (Civil Defense), Feb. 2018. Available at https://commons.wikimedia.org/wiki/File:Kalapana,_HI,_county_parking,_start_of_the_lava_trail_2018-Feb-3.jpg

provide safe access to viewing the active lava flow and were first set up in 2002 when the flow from entered the ocean (Hawaiian Volcano Observatory n.d.). As the flow changed over the years, these lava-viewing areas dynamically responded and shifted in their position to the flowing lava. Developing as communities in and of themselves, with a population present of and for the visiting public, the evolving nature of these areas correlates with their usage. Positioned to emulate the national park's designated areas for optimal viewing, the county designated hours for the county's manning of these public areas, set aside parking areas, and public access for optimal viewing within a safe distance to the present hazards. Once parked (arriving in personal car or by tourist van or bus), visitors often traversed on foot out over lava fields to see the molten glow more clearly. Most recently, visitors used bicycles to ride the 4-mile gravel road to the end of the viewing area over the cooled fields of black lava. Visitors can also visit the more remote Puʻu ʻŌʻō vent by driving to the end of local Route 130 and parking at the gravel lot provided by the Hawai'i County Civil Defense Agency. Once parked, visitors could walk a total of 8 miles over cooled lava fields towards the lava's ocean entry and back to the parking lot while seeing the lava's glow the entire time. The walk could also be accessed from inside the national park with roughly the equivalent distance in and out.

Recently, as noted in the August 13, 2017, *Hawaii Tribune Herald*, entry to the pathway out to see the lava had become a site rich with "entrepreneurial spirit". As Kristen Johnson (2017) notes, hot dog stands, bicycle rental vendors, and other food and consumable vendors (local artists), have set up shop each night for a piece of the pie that is offered by the typical 900 visitors coming to the lava-viewing areas during the hours of 2–10 pm (Johnson). Hawai'i County Civil Defense Administrator Talmadge Magno noted that these vendors are compliant with the state's Department of Taxation to ensure proper permitting and licensing of vendors for purposes of public safety (Johnson 2017). Places to park at the lava-viewing areas also served as a profit maker for local residents, with one example a cardboard sign that advertised "$20 VIP Lava Parking" in one resident's lot located near the lava-viewing area entrance. Of particular irony is law's inability to fully regulate residential profiteers, such as this particular parking space, as the County does not own all visited land. Nonetheless, the "burned out medical assistant" turned hot dog saleswoman asserted that she was doing a greater public service to those who visited the spectacle by feeding them hot dogs (sometimes up to 60 dogs and burgers per night) and "helping people in a different aspect" (Johnson 2017). At Kalapana each night, the spectacle was therefore twofold, with the glowing lava flowing into the ocean and also the emerging "goldrush" that has resulted from hungry visitors who consume hot dogs and rent bikes to go and see the glow. The experience is untamed wildness rich with unregulatable natural and human activity in an area roughly 25 miles from Hilo, the nearest city.

Law is limited in its ability to regulate. Through the setting up of frameworks of regulation, the impetus for compliance exists as the expectation of risk is quite high (O'Malley 2004). However, in the case of the hot dog vendor, would this risk carry beyond the visible glow of distant lava to ensure that the hot dogs are fully cooked and edible according to federal food safety guidelines? What then is the focus of the public safety here? Interestingly, the regulation seemed more concerned with the spectacle of governing to ensure that the lava and its viewing were managed rather than the experience of safety whether through proper food handling procedures or making sure that the bikes (as well as the bike vendors) are in proper working order.

An ongoing critique of the public's lack of engagement in the 2018 Leilani eruption was that the County of Hawai'i did not set up the same type of lava-viewing areas as had previously existed. The local public was kept from viewing these lava flows, even as the national and international media was permitted to go beyond the restricted areas within the subdivision of Leilani Estates as patrolled by the Hawai'i National Guard. Yet, other ways that had existed previously prior to the Leilani eruption also existed in 2018. One of these was viewing the lava's entry into the ocean from lava-viewing boats. Lava boat tours were quite popular with those wishing to visit the spectacle. With the water space regulated by the U.S. Coast Guard, some boats got very close to the ocean entry where giant steam clouds billowed thousands of feet into the sky and molten lava exploded once the heated rock hit the cool ocean water. One boat was at the wrong place at the wrong time, despite being allowed by the Coast Guard to boat in so close to the action, as an exploding lava bomb cascaded through the air and crashed through the boat's tin roof and onto the passengers below (Jacobs 2018). The Civil Defense determined that the Coast Guard had been routinely allowing boats within too close of proximity to the exploding lava (Boyette 2018).

Public quality of disaster/public quality of spectacle

Outside the United States (and perhaps including Iceland), volcanoes can be climbed with visitors often getting in the way of explosive events (such as Japan in September 2014 and more recently in Italy in January 2018). This is indicative of the larger framework of an Americanized law that governs over rather than through. Common sense is portrayed as something that flies in the face of law and order. In the United States, common sense, because it happens on the level of the individual, is portrayed as a threat to the order that comes from the uniformity and normativity that happens when law paternalizes behavior, risk, and response. This is evident in the paradox of the Civil Defense's lava-viewing areas. In these areas, law is only present during business hours (until 10 pm). Although the presence of law is conveyed through fences and signs, common sense of a visiting (and curious) public takes over and trumps the paternalistic normativity that law attempts through manning the area with law enforcement personnel. What then does law really look like? How do we know this is a legally managed landscape, or lavascape? What does the lavascape look like?

Moving beyond the safe confines of seeing lava glow from within the national park at the Jaggar Museum Overlook at Halema'uma'u Crater, lava oozed beyond federal jurisdiction from the southeastern flank of Kīlauea at Pu'u 'Ō'ō vent and into the Pacific Ocean at Kamokuna under local jurisdiction during the thirty-year eruption as well as in the 2018 Leilani eruption. As such, the lavascape shows us that human-made law is compelled to respond rather than to dictate the kineticism of law. However, law within the lavascape is visibly operationalized in a variety of ways. One such way is the ability to view lava as seen from the air. Helicopters could routinely fly the visiting public over the erupting lava until the airspace over the Leilani eruption was restricted in 2018. Prior to 2018, many of these helicopters for tourists were flown by private helicopter companies. Other helicopters provide scientific data about the lava flow. Others flew over to collect news and media information.

However, during the Leilani eruption, even as the general (and local) public were curfewed, if not restricted during the flow; however, media personnel were allowed in by the Civil Defense. This level of access seems to position the viewing of the lava spectacle as privatized, in the sense that access is open to a limited and select public represented by reporters with camera footage. Yet for a different understanding of public access, namely through gate entry to the national park, access is not free and costs each entering vehicle. However, outside the national park in the Civil Defense lava-viewing areas, public access by car and foot to lava was encouraged through paved parking lots for cars and pedestrian walkways for visitors. This difference between the Leilani flow and flows prior to 2018 rested with law's attempt to manage access to the spectacle of flowing lava. However, this management even then was not *in perpetua*, or all the time. Instead, there were certain hours that guard stations were manned with available parking personnel help to direct traffic and Civil Defense officers present at these lava-viewing areas. These limited hours were the result of public monies allotted for this purpose and ironically invited an "after hours" contingency of people who sought closer proximity to the active lava under the cover of darkness and when the glow was most spectacular.

Whether by air (helicopter tours or drones), by sea (boat tours that view the lava from the ocean), or by land (at overlooks or in the lava field), molten lava could be seen by sightseers through legal as well as illegal means. From the air, sightseers could pay for private helicopter or airplane rides to fly over the lava. Drones were even a possibility to fly over this volcanic airspace to capture footage of bubbling lava. However, during the Leilani flow, a temporary flight restriction was ordered by the Federal Aviation Administration (FAA) on behalf of Hawai'i County officials to curb unrestrained flight activity over the flow. As a result, public overview flights involving helicopters, planes, and/or drones were restricted while private groups such as local legislators, politicians, scientists, researchers, the military, and emergency management personnel were allowed access.

From the ocean, sightseers could see the lava as it spilled steaming into the waves. Lava boat tours with paying passengers could travel from local harbors in Hilo to the coastal lava entries to view the spectacle. Similarly, private boaters could also travel to see the glow of the lava. Once the Leilani eruption started in May 2018 however, the U.S. Coast Guard implemented and enforced a barrier around the spectacle known as the Lava Entry Safety Zone. In July 2018, the perimeter guidelines were relaxed by the Coast Guard for specified research and commercial boats, including some lava boat tours (Boyette 2018). Tragically, one such vessel ventured too close for safety and was sprayed with chunks of molten lava. Twenty-three passengers were injured as hot glowing lava landed on the boat. Since the accident, the full depth of the Lava Entry Safety Zone for sightseeing was once again enforced due to the unpredictability of lava entering the ocean.

From the land, lava could be legally viewed from the organized setting of the rockwalls and ropes set up on the crater's rim at the Jaggar Museum Overlook in the national park or through the lava-viewing areas set up and managed by the Hawai'i County Civil Defense. These areas were complete with parking lots and enforcement personnel making the witnessing of the glow of molten lava a legally encouraged, managed, and monitored activity. Such sightseeing was legal as the viewing itself was a sanctioned and legally supported activity. At other areas where lava was erupting, the National Guard–manned roadblocks to prevent sightseeing access. Because of the distinctions between legal and illegal viewing, authority over sightseeing is authority over the spectacle with law asserting control over the spectacle. Whether as the Coast Guard manning ocean viewing, the Hawai'i National Guard patrolling access to lava flowing over land in Leilani, or controlling access in lava-viewing areas, the presence of law itself becomes a spectacle of control.

Yet, despite law's attempt to control the seeing of the spectacle, lava was also illegally viewable. For example, sightseers could wait until the Civil Defense officers at the lava-viewing areas went home for the night, usually around ten o'clock, and then trek across the lava fields to get closer to the molten lava. Another avenue might be to gather a group of sightseers and take them either by land or by boat through unsanctioned methods to see the lava close up. These unpermitted lava tours existed outside regulatory boundaries or legally approved directives. In fact, for some, that was the point. Sneaking in past boundaries set up by either the military or Civil

Defense, the allure of seeing the lava' glow was heightened through illegal access to the spectacle. Called Lava Loiters (Wu 2018), these folks ignored the roadblocks and engaged in heightened personal risk to witness the glow. According to the Hawai'i State Department of Land and Natural Resources, "Since the beginning of the current eruption in early May, nearly 90 people have been cited. Under an emergency proclamation from Governor Ige, potential fines and jail time for anyone convicted of loitering in the eruption zone could be as high as $5,000 and one year in jail" (Big Island Video News 2018(a)).

The legal spectacle of guarding the lava and preventing illegal lava access reveals law's incomplete quest to be in control of an unpredictable and uncontrollable environment. Even though law permitted the preapproved sightseeing to capture imagery of Kīlauea's landscape in ways that were limited in scope and granted selectively to the media, politicians, and scientists, images on social media appeared from people who transgressed the boundaries to take their own photographs. Indicative of these errant sightseers, the absence of available public viewing during the Leilani flow became a point of local critique as no lava view areas had been set up (even as of this article's writing in December 2018) (Big Island Video News 2018 (b)). Yet even while the glow prevailed, sightseers were able to drive to distant hilly outlooks in neighboring towns and neighborhoods of East Hawai'i and witness the fountaining of Fissure 8. In the early days of the eruption, some also watched from their own front yards, as many did not evacuate until the lava actually permeated the boundaries of their homes and yards.

The legal semiotics of sightseeing in the lavascape are therefore representative of law itself. Whether as physical structures (ropes and rock walls at the Jaggar Museum overlook) or as the jurisdictional display of the military as physical barriers (National Guard personnel stationed at roadblocks or Coast Guard boats at ocean entries and in the waters near the flow), law is symbolic in its regulation of sightseeing. Physical restrictions on sightseeing are commonly justified through calls for safety with affirmations of common sense that also reveal law's perceptive domain of responsibility over chaos. When the lava tour boat was hit by flying lava, Wil Okabe, Hawai'i County Manager, who was unaware of the relaxed Coast Guard perimeter restrictions, noted, "The lava in the ocean is very unpredictable. If that particular tour boat had gone several feet to the right, that explosion would have gone into the hull instead of the roof," Okabe said. "It's a very unpredictable situation. It's very dangerous" (Boyette 2018). Even through law's restrictions, chaos ensued.

Another example of law's inability to contain chaos was the parking lot with guard shack at the lava-viewing areas. This guard shack represents a legal semiotic of access. In the parking lot, law's preference for vehicular-based sightseeing tethered cars and passengers to temporary visitation as people would drive in, park and see the spectacle, and then leave the area.

Yet, we know that the semiotic of the unmanned guard shack served almost as invitation to the sightseeing public once the guards had left for the night.

Another semiotic of access was the buzzing of helicopters above the fissures in Leilani Estates throughout the summer. These aircraft signified the heights of power, insofar as the link between allowance and prestige was limited to officially sanctioned viewing. Local legislators and politicians flew over the Leilani eruption in order to better comprehend the extent of the flow and to then subsequently offer words of wisdom. The positionality of local politicians to offer expertise through privileged sightseeing was considered the foundation for generating relevant legislation insofar as "seeing is believing."[5] While scientifically generated overflights seemed commonplace and reasonable, flights made by politicians, who were from the state but who were not actually residentially based on Hawai'i Island, seemed to be a privileged form of sightseeing and representative of voyeuristic intrusion into the spectacle denied local viewing.

While the ability to see lava first hand during the Leilani flow was a restricted privilege, the images that recorded the lava's activity during this time were available nationally and internationally. As such, the local semiotic of seeing the lava was reserved for officially sanctioned sightseers (media, politicians, scientists) with local residents unable to see the spectacle transpiring in their own community as lava-viewing areas were not available and lava loiters were criminalized. Local residents could only see what was happened on their island from television stations and newspapers, whose reporters were allowed into the flow for the purpose of taking pictures. Pictures and photographs that were managed by the comparatively few local residents who posted on social media were quickly taken out of the public domain and snatched up by media companies or by individual photographers. In this way, the image of molten lava is a semiotic of governance and access to this legalized spectacle in the lavascape is discursively framed as a narrative of visual authority officially sanctioning the lava's path and possible impact to the select few. Even through the legal semiotic of images, the legal spectacle at Kīlauea was rife with chaos and disorder despite the attempted management of such an eruptive environment.

Notes

1 Fissure 8 is a title generated by convenience and it serves as eruptive placeholder until a formal name can be given by Hawaiian elders and community leaders.

2 During this same time, I convened the 16th Roundtable for the Semiotics of Law, held at Kīlauea Military Camp inside the Hawai'i Volcanoes National Park. We really couldn't have timed it any better, as the lava flowed over Halema'uma'u Crater that same weekend. What a treat, as we essentially had front row seats to this rare spectacle. Mahalo, Tutu Pele!

3 According to the figures published by the Hawai'i Volcanoes National Park (released April 28, 2016, available at https://www.nps.gov/havo/learn/news/20160428_pr_visitation.htm), visitation to the park is increasing: 1,832,660 visitors in 2015; 1,693,005 visitors in 2014; 1,583,209 visitors in 2013 (source: https://www.nps.gov/havo/learn/news/2013visitation.htm).

4 Ibid., p. 30.

5 Initially, I spoke informally in a personal conversation with Representative Chris Todd of the Hawai'i State Legislature; later, this was further supported by video footage from Senator Kaiali'i Kahele (Hawaii State Legislature) as posted on "Aerial View of Lava Flow in Leilani Estates, May 29" on the *Star Advertiser*'s website: http://www.staradvertiser.com/2018/05/29/photo-galleries/aerial-view-lava-flow-leilani-estates-may-29/ (Accessed 17 December 2018).

Chapter 4

Topologies of governance

Various stages of movement characterize the dynamic landscape. Each stage is temporally distinct with specific qualities that spatially define the stage of movement. For example, these stages of movement at Strokkur Geyser (in Icelandic, *strokkur* means "to churn") range from quiet and steaming to eruptive and fountaining and then back to quiet and steaming. Here, the temporality of this dynamic landscape can even be timed with an eruption timed to occur every 4 to 10 minutes. In contrast, the gushing of boiling water from inside the earth occurs every 60–100 minutes at Old Faithful in Yellowstone National Park. At the geyser, the timing of when the next eruption is expected to occur generates a spatial understanding of possibility and likelihood of the environment that is demarcated through ropes and signs. Yet, even without such overt markers, the steam rising from the ground on a consistent basis gives rise (literally) to the feeling of expectation and measured caution. Steam rising from the ground indicates heated action below the surface and the possibility of explosion similar to the action of water boiling in a pot on the stove. Timing such an eruption creates a sense of control over what otherwise would be considered unpredictable. The presumption of prediction based on the eruptive cycle of the past is used to predict the future. Hence, the temporality of timing the eruptions from geysers conveys a sense of reliance and dependency on the human framing of nature itself. While geysers themselves cannot be truly regulated and ultimately retain autonomy over their own activity, the expected schedule of eruptive events predicting the heated surge of water reveals human attempts to be in charge of nature through prediction. Besides, how much fun is it to clock nature?

At Kīlauea, the stages of movement are catalogued as an attempt to describe, if not position, the otherwise wild activities of the volcano; unfortunately, the eruption of volcanoes is much less straightforward than the eruption of geysers. In this dynamic landscape, the volatility of the earth's movement is layered and complex as the spatio-temporal aspects of this volcano seem to take a path of waking up, dancing, and then resting. In the quiet and glowing stage, one can see the distant glow of molten rock deep within Halema'uma'u Crater. In the active (molten), yet contained stage, actual bubbling lava can be seen just below the rim of Halema'uma'u Crater and contained within the crater walls. The active (molten) and creeping stage is when lava first oozes from vents on the flanks of the mountain opening up the flow of lava. The active (molten) and raging stage is what happens when lava gains speed to flow like water in rivers of molten lava traveling to the ocean. In a more vertical fashion, the active (molten) and fountaining stage happens when lava fountains upwards with a visual similar to the fountaining of a geyser. The quiet and cooling stage of movement is when the volume of lava flowing from the earth slows and is no longer active as the eruption is near its end. Lastly, the cooled (yet still quite hot) and hardened stage is when lava no longer flows, or even moves, but is beginning the months-long and sometimes years-long process of fully cooling. Examples of each state provide an aesthetic that reveals the complexity of a landscape in motion in which the ebbs and flows of terrain sculpt the heterotemporality of eruption, the materiality of lava, and the layering of land and legality.

Ebbs and flows of terrain

Mapping projects of the terrain attempt to capture the topographies of landscape through visual representation. This visual framing of law and place charts the physical qualities of land, but can also record the political, historical, and cultural aspects of spatiality inherent to a particular place. Whether mapping wilderness or managed land, the mapping of hazard and land ownership generates ontological dimensions of man's relationship to environment. Often, this relationship is linear (Ingold 2007) with borders as structures of division. Because lines are never simply linear, the constructed areas on either side of lines engenders a zone, or a borderland (Jones 2012; Jones 2016; Dudziak and Volpp 2006) which muddies the meaning and purpose of a line. While the types of borders may visibly vary, the meaning of borders creates a zone of understanding in which crossing becomes a process. No longer clean and neat, the crossing of borders in a mapped dynamic landscape can be confused and unkempt (Law 2004). Lava is an example of such an unkempt border as the chaos created as it flows over the landscape is neither neat nor clean and perpetually generates and redefines the borders previously mapped while challenging their predicted future.

The management of nature transpires through mapping. The process of making the unorganized legible (Scott 1998) is a project of order and governance over nature. Through mapping, the unpredictable is delineated and marked, the predictable assuredly presented as fact, and the unknown is no longer unknown. As legal metaphor, mapping projects relieve the disarray of the unsurveyed and chart the landscape through authority and prediction. Just as the law maps the terrain of the everyday landscape through traffic signs (Wagner 2006), parking spaces (Marusek 2020), and roads (Seo 2019), the cadastral maps of past, present, and future lava flows depict the kineticism of a landscape in motion.

The scope of mapping at Kīlauea, whether as the Lava Zone Map or the ongoing mapping of active and/or historical lava flows, is the visualization of law's response to the politics of hazard. Mapping potential threat of lava inundation or mapping historical flows is an attempt to control future unpredictability. In this way, lava-mapping projects position the map as a legal semiotic in which prediction aligns with historical reality. However, these maps also serve as cultural semiotic of understanding and negotiating life on the slopes on actively volcanic terrain. As such, the map distills ignorance in lieu of visually constructed knowledge of the volcano's past behavior and likely future performance. Such mapping projects and the maps that are generated are a function of a responsive governance but also serve to compel law's responsibility in generating the map for public knowledge. Even as the map may not be the territory (Hayakawa as quoted in Brigham 2009), mapped and mappable lava activity propel law's authority to map (through the selected formal recognition of some maps over others) even as it limits legal culpability through representation instead of fact. Maps are spatio-temporal interpretations of landscapes in terms of predictions and realities that change even as the interpretations of the process of mapping also changes. In this way, landscapes can be in motion in and of themselves, but also in terms of their representation. We know this to be political insofar as the mapping of motion is a project of governance (Barr 2016) that constructs identities and defines contested relationships to power. These "interstitial zones of hybridization" (Dudziak and Volpp 2006, 3) catalyze a discourse of watching and living with risk through forecast, public awareness, and technologies of surveillance, such as webcams at the volcano's rim. This technique of governance provides a practice of mapping that becomes normalized (Scott 1998) as a tool of the state to maintain control over nature and have a grip on hazards and potential threat.

Mapping projects attempt to make the abstract visible, as the visual technique of governance is the ordered management of the wild. At Kīlauea, the abstract mapping of future lava flows is generated from past flows in what's known as the USGS Lava Zone Map. This system of ranking was first generated in 1974 by the United States Geological Survey (USGS) and was based upon long-term lava flows (Wright et al. 1992) with information gathered from scientific data concerning the age of lava drawn from written records beginning in the 1800s and Hawaiian oral traditions. Because the map is intended for long-term probability, the USGS Lava Zone Map is not revised after new eruptions. While this map interprets future risk from past eruptions, the map also serves as a vital source of knowledge for local real estate.

The prediction of where lava is predicted to flow next is described as zones of risk. In the Lava Zone Map (see Figure 4.1 on the next page), Hawai'i Island is mapped according to level of recent activity and severity of

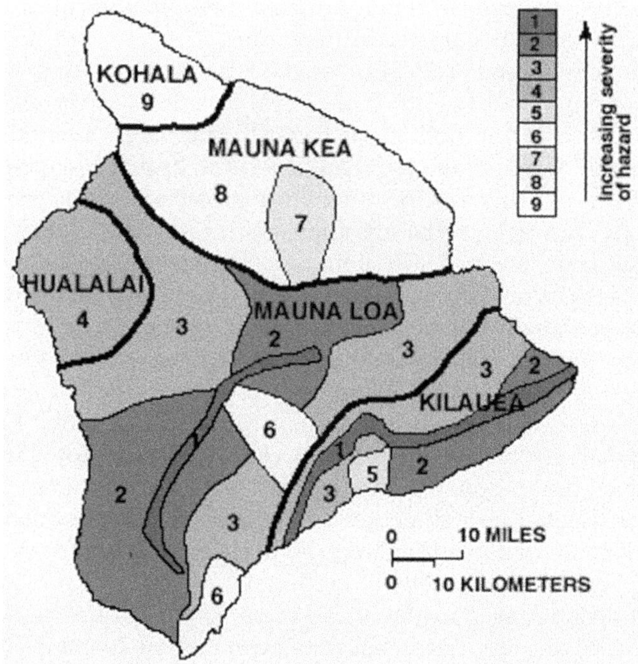

Figure 4.1 USGS Hawai'i Island lava hazard map. Available at https://commons.wikimedia.org/wiki/File:USGS_Hawaii_Island_Lava_Hazard_Map.giff

predicted risk from each of the island's five volcanoes, outlined in solid dark lines, with projected and actual areas of historical lava flow activity. With the least risk, Lava Zone 9 borders Kohala Volcano, which erupted over 60,000 years ago. With the most risk, Mauna Loa and Kīlauea, with rift zones in Lava Zone 1, have erupted most recently and in the case of Kīlauea, is still steaming at the time of this writing in 2020. Lava Zones 1–3, with the highest risk of inundation, includes the land surrounding Kīlauea ranging from the Hawai'i Volcanoes National Park (HVNP) and neighboring residential subdivisions in the District of Puna. Mauna Loa, erupting in 1984, but constantly rumbling and currently under the mid-level "advisory" level from Hawaiian Volcano Observatory (HVO), also involves Lava Zones 1–3. The purple strips of Lava Zone 1 indicate the areas of highest risk known as Rift Zones, or where active lava is most likely to flow.

According to Hawaiian Volcano Observatory (n.d.), these zones are mapped according to the percentage of area covered by lava flows since 1800 as well as in the last 750 years. Designation for these zones is based on geologic mapping and dating of older flows, but also from historic eruptions described in written records dating from the 1800s as well as from Hawaiian oral tradition passed down through the generations. Just as topographic features of island terrain are taken into account, so is the repetitive nature of lava flows to take similar paths to earlier eruptions. Knowledge about the land is the source of knowledge for how each volcano is likely to behave and tethers indigenous ways of knowing to scientific understanding of collected data.

The availability of Lava Zone Map as a dependable source of landscape topography in this volcanic terrain results in the collaborative communication between science and culture as geology and oral tradition work together to generated predictive models for future lava activity. However, the Lava Zone Map is also a source of legal governance as the map is used to gauge insurance costs for individual homes and subdivision-based neighborhoods through real estate sales and land contracts. In this way, the governance of risk from lava inundation is scientific, cultural, historical, as well as legal. Even as Lava Zones 1, 2, and 3 host the majority of island residents in the populated areas of the southern Kona Coast, Ocean View and the Ka'u district, the Puna subdivisions, as well in Keaau, many residential home insurers will not grant policies to homes in Lava Zone 1 and occasionally to homes in Lava Zone 2.

As noted earlier, lava oozes across the landscape with the generally, slow-moving risk of lava crossing the land. On Kīlauea and Mauna Loa, two of the most heavily studied volcanoes in the world, lava risk is constantly monitored by scientific agencies as the USGS and the HVO that convey levels of monitored risk assessment to Hawai'i Island County government agencies, who in turn, monitor possibilities of risk to those in populated areas. The possibility of future lava flow as premised on past models means that legally, the assumption of the risk when assumed by insurance companies, allows for higher rates if there is available coverage in the first place. Many insurance companies from the U.S. mainland refuse to insure residents of Lava Zones 1 and 2, which opens up a local market for property insurance. Local knowledge in this case prioritizes the historical ebbs and flows of lava on the island and is subsequently another way in which cultural knowledge serves as a nonlegal actor and source of law. James Scott (1998, 24) describes such a relationship as "a pattern of relations between local knowledge and practices on one hand and state administrative routines on the other." The Lava Zone Map represents a "tool of legibility" (Scott 1998, 25) that unlike the failed measures of state action in Scott's work, may actually assist residents and local government in channeling scientific study into figuring out where the flow is likely to go next. Such maps also stimulate the local economy in terms of local real estate knowledge and insurance practices. Yet, as even another type of local knowledge, indigenous historical accounts recognize that the lava is likely to erupt in particular areas and with noted frequency. Living too close to an active volcano might prove hazardous to both property and person.

Heterotemporality of eruption

Just as lava oozes, time also oozes. As time happens in the present, so too does it happen in the future. While warning and risk are predicted for the future, both are discussed in present terms, as based upon, in part, on what's happened in the past. In other words, predictability of the future is determined by the past as well as what's occurring in the present. The timing of events within the dynamic landscape can be mapped after the fact, or once the rate of speed from flowing nature has stopped, as a way to method of forecasting the future. The visual representation of past activity is used as a tool for thinking about the future. Yet, maps are frozen in time once they are drawn, even as the date and time of a map may change at any time once that area is mapped.

Similar to the seeming stillness of the lava within Halema'uma'u Crater, Strokkur Geyser seems passive when it is not erupting. When the water does shoot from the earth, we understand the event through a timed prediction of when the cycle of eruption will take place next and for how long (signs that are placed near the opening of the geyser describe this timing). Albeit over longer increments, even time is measured at Kīlauea, as the speed of lava flows can be mapped, as shown in Figure 4.2.

The speed of a lava flow is dependent upon whether or not that flow is covering new ground, or whether it is traveling over previously inundated land. Other variable factors include the type of lava (the faster ‘a'ā or the slower pāhoehoe), the rate of eruption, the duration of the eruption, as well as the topography of the land over which the lava flows, taking into account slope, the presence of lava tubes and/or channels, as well as other directions the flow may decide to either follow or create anew. The speed of lava (specifically from a 1950 Mauna Loa flow) has been clocked at 9.3 km/5.8 mi per hour, and was assessed as “slightly slower than typical human jogging speed” (Hawaiian Volcano Observatory, n.d. (2)). Jack Thompson's comment from chapter one that he could “outrun” Madame Pele may be more factual than flippant.

Time is an element that is not as clearly measured at the volcano as it is at the geyser, even if movements of the volcano are measured through seismograph measuring the movement of the earth as well as through the visual monitoring of the lava's height within the crater and accompanying geographic cycles of inflation and deflation. The prediction of the next lava flow is influenced by the heightened measured movement of the terrain, such as through increased earthquakes as the earthquake map from the HVO in Figure 4.3 shows. In the limited snippet of geologic time referred to as February 2020 when this map was recorded, Mauna Loa is much more active than Kīlauea:

Eruptions from volcanoes are clearly not as easily timed as those from geysers. In contrast to the geyser's movement (eruptions) that occur with enough

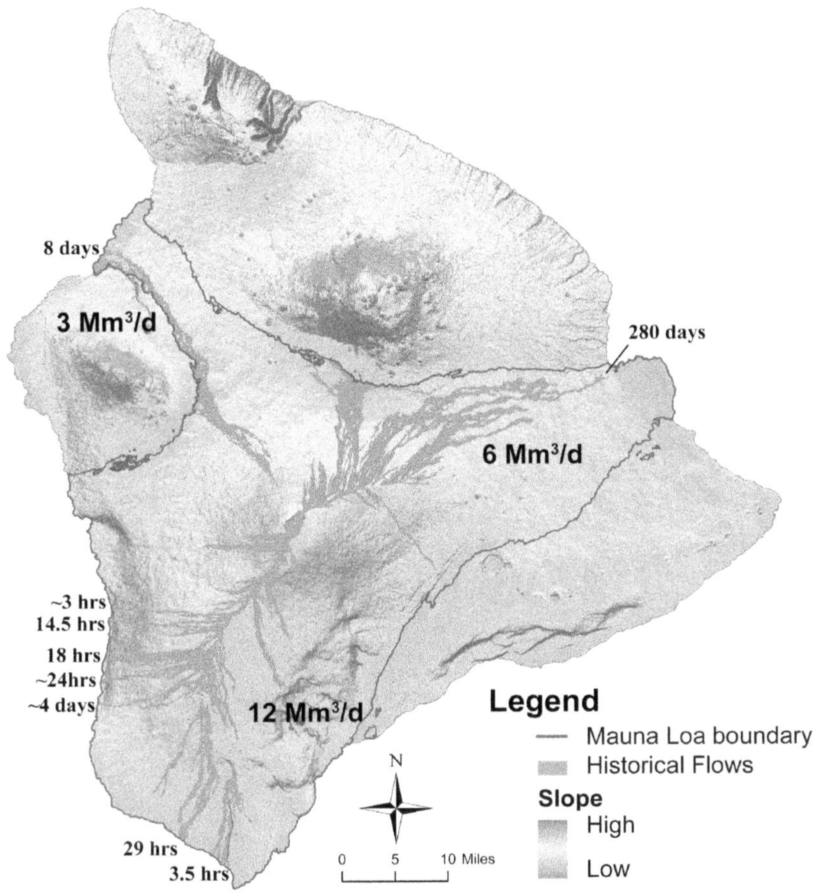

Figure 4.2 Lava flow travel times based on actual flow rates.

Source: https://volcanoes.usgs.gov/observatories/hvo/hawaii_lava_flows.html

regular frequency to be tracked, the eruption of lava, or even the rise and fall of its glow, are not on a schedule. As a liquid that flows but also as a solid that hardens, lava is a fluid object (Law and Singleton 2005, 338) "because it flows and *gently* changes shape, bit by bit." Like lava, law, too, oozes, in and out of boundaries. Like the flow of water, law "produces an ever shifting medium through which the 'production of locality' is enabled (Appadurai and Breckenridge 2009). Lava is a legal metaphor for law's fluidity.

As a spectacle of governance, law adapts to the dynamic landscape and kinetically responds to contextually specific environments as a testament of its durability. Neither static nor stagnant, regulation of the natural

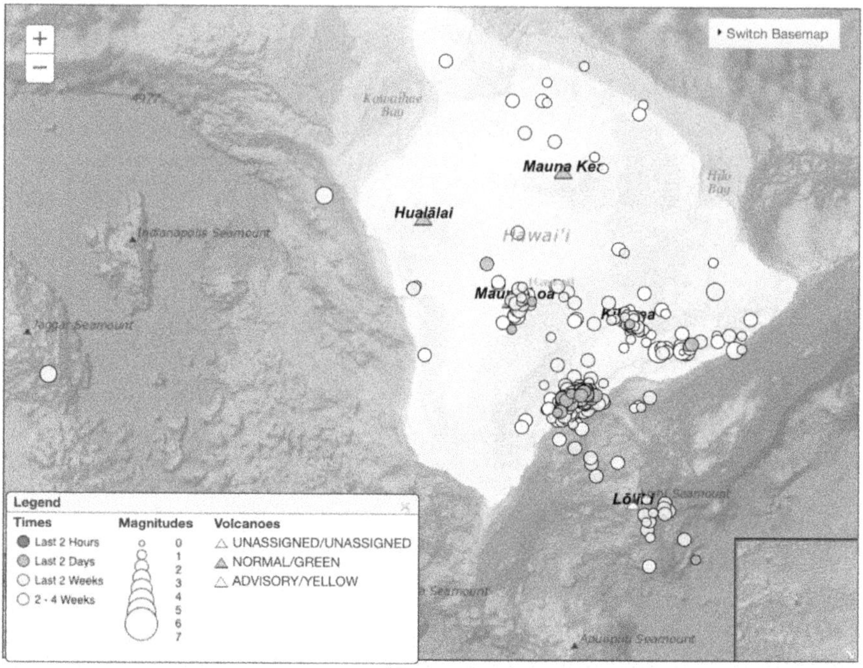

Figure 4.3 HVO earthquake map.

Source: https://volcanoes.usgs.gov/observatories/hvo/hvo_earthquakes.html

environment is socially and culturally generated, and as such, is fluid in context and application. The context of mapping makes the experienced legible by the state (Scott 1998) and through time, able to be tracked. In this way, those who govern are able to visibly present the image of order through the mapped landscape in such a way as to present the landscape that is in motion instead to be a landscape in which that motion is much less visible. The map is the rendering of a static landscape, taken as a snapshot at a certain time in history. Through the trapping of the land's motion, law, as the source of the mapping, represents a government that presents itself as in control of the movement. Even as the timing of images changes, the image itself is a static representation of terrain at that moment. Prediction is a fluid attempt at the perpetuation of order. The mapping of time and place allows for the legal representation of nature at stages of action, whether through ongoing GPS-mapping projects (Turner, Perroy and Hon 2017) or maps that appear in stages. Maps in real time can be interactive, as the earthquake map website depicts, but real time can also be understood as according to stages in time.

The heterotemporality of eruption is shown on maps that vary according to the timeframe in which they are recorded. Whether as a method of tracking the movement of flow and the resultant lava inundation, or as a way to track the lava itself, the visual image captures a particular context at a particular time. Yet, in other maps, such as the map in Figure 4.4, time can be visualized according to the distance advanced by accumulated lava. In this way, the heterotemporality of eruption is less horizontal, as in Figure 4.5, and much more vertical as the height, or thickness, of the lava is measured. The flow can be visually depicted as a fluid motion of the months of lava flow activity, as the red on the map indicate. In other words, we can see through the red and the mapped thickness of this land that the water presents an obstacle and boundary to the flow of lava over the land. At the red borders of the flow, the lava seems to have slowed and piled up to become the extensive thickness for which it is mapped and therefore significant. The thickness of the lava represents the thickness of time in which the materiality of a slowed lava flow shows the varying speeds that characterize the kinetic landscape. Through Bakhtin's discussion of chronotopes, Mariana Valverde (2014, 53) considers the spread between space and time in terms of "spatiotemporalization processes in a pluralistic and dynamic manner." Through these maps, the kinetic materiality of the eruption is visualized.

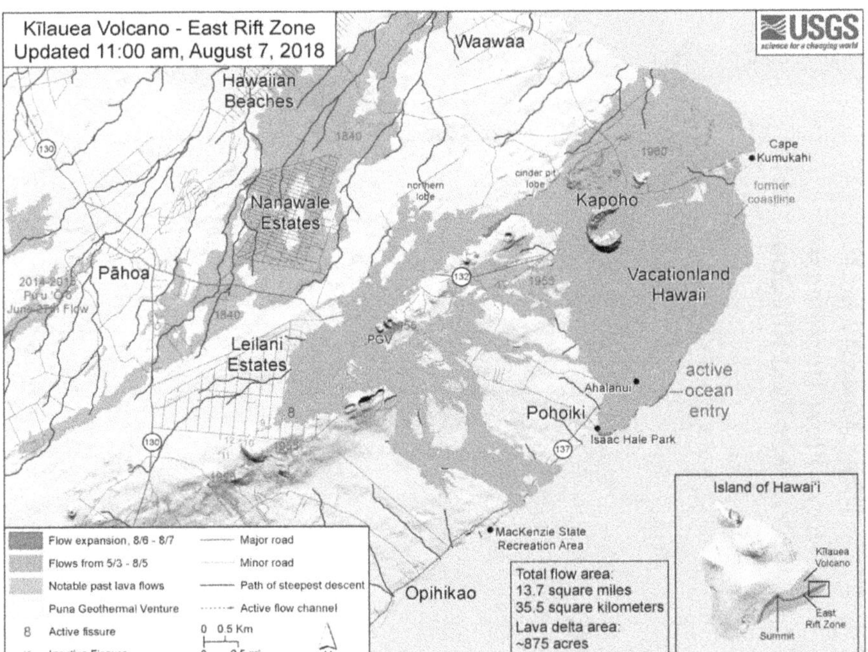

Figure 4.4 Lava flow thickness map.

Source: https://volcanoes.usgs.gov/observatories/hvo/maps_uploads/image-545.jpg

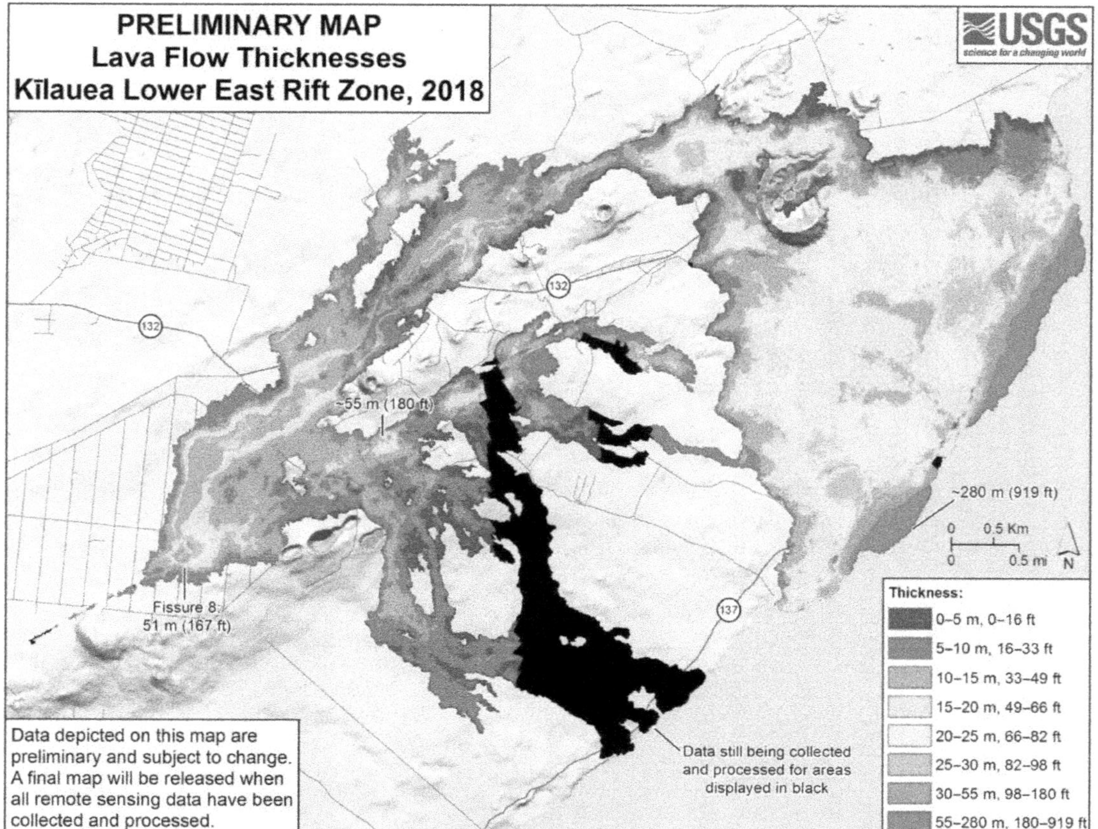

Figure 4.5 Kīlauea Volcano – East Rife Zone, August 7, 2018.

Source: https://volcanoes.usgs.gov/observatories/hvo/maps_uploads/image-539.jpg

Yet, the mapping of time is as much a scientific project, as it is a legal project. Prediction and warning assist the ability of law to assert a sense of temporal ownership over past volcanic movement through the practice of tracking a terrain's movement. This ability to govern the landscape through mapping is a project of order with ramifications for the movement of people, the terrain of public lands, and the private purchasing of real estate, particularly in Lava Zones 1 and 2. The dynamic nature of mapping the kinetic terrain in the Kīlauea region of Hawai'i Island is an ongoing, continual practice, as the following map, with accompanying disclaimer from the Hawai'i County Civil Defense Agency, reveals:

> Disclaimer (with a box to check to "agree" in order to gain access to the map/site):
>
> This site was designed to provide quick and easy access to the records and maps for properties located in the County of Hawai'i. Listed information does not include all of the information about every property located in this county. The information on this site is subject to daily changes. Users must understand that the information and descriptions may change at any time. Persons using this data should NOT rely upon this information in formulating important decisions that affect their financial future nor should this information be considered as legal documentation. No warranties, expressed or implied, are provided for the data herein, its use or its interpretation. Utilization of the search facility indicates understanding and acceptance of this statement by the user. Thank you very much.

The possibility, if not likelihood, of change to the terrain from future eruptions is the challenge to a static rendering of the landscape. Through this disclaimer, law purports itself to be the source of financial stability in terms of real estate transactions, but concurrently escapes formal responsibility if the lines on the maps change. In other words, legal authority to render an official rendering of legal terrain is challenged by the terrain itself once it moves. The map is merely an approximation, just as law's performativity is illusory insofar as law is not an exact science and depends upon nonlegal actors for its identity and ability to govern through mapping. Yet, in such mapping projects, scientific actors such as the USGS or Geographic Information System (GIS) systems with drones flown by university professors with information publicly disseminated by the Civil Defense is more to *frame* and *show* rather than to clearly demarcate in a fluid manner as eruption happens, as indicated by the disclaimer. The discursive context of the mappability of moving terrain positions law to be in charge, even as the maps themselves are expected to change.

Drones provide the bird's eye perspective through vertical viewing and mapping from above. In fact, the legalized demarcation of hazardous terrain is financially governed by property insurers using the Lava Zone Map in determining a plot's proximity to the volcanic rift zone. Buyers are warned about the likelihood of future eruptions when purchasing property in Lava Zones 1 and 2. For Kīlauea, the East Rift Zone is the most likely and most-recurrent area for lava flows as based upon historical flows and current prediction. Therefore, the periodic mapping and active prediction of the dynamic landscape of Kīlauea is the mapping of order with the purpose of attempting to provide social stability, legal protectionism, and limits to actual state liability. In these maps, the management of nature is a legal metaphor for the management of potential chaos that itself is mapped according to areas of risk and frameworks of hazard. Movement of the earth is tracked and coded according to these mapping projects.

However, the heterotemporality of eruption in using modern maps as topographies of governance is a relatively recent enterprise. Maps now stand in for what formerly might have been considered to be common sense insofar as it was obvious where the lava has flowed and where it was likely to flow next based simply on the visible layout of the land itself. It is clear that human presence on the dynamic landscape of Kīlauea has existed long before the volcano itself was mapped. Prior to mapping the daily activity of Kīlauea, the practice of waiting for activity to occur supplanted the practice of prediction. Mapping projects (Coombes et al. 2012) and the chronopolitical matrix (Klinke 2012) are themselves a way to map law's attempted ownership over the dynamism of nature. Mapping is a way to see postcolonial spaces that include nature, such as that within the jurisdiction of the HVNP, but also the land under the contemporary jurisdiction of Hawai'i Island.

These areas, formerly undeveloped lava fields, were the source of intense land speculation and development marketed the U.S. mainland during the 1950s (Cooper and Daws 1985). Even during the most recent eruption in 2018, Hawai'i Island Harry Kim did not want to restrict construction in Lava Zones 1 and 2 because so much real estate transpired here: "These are our bedroom communities. A lot of people live there because that's the only place they can afford" (Lauer 2018). Or, as residents who returned to the Kalapana Gardens subdivision, inundated by lava in 2012, and rebuilt a new house stated, "Where else in Hawaii can you buy land with an ocean view like this for $10,000?" (Helsel and Calabrese 2018).

In considering these mapped areas as the visual representations of the nomosphere (Delaney 2010), the layers of jurisdiction reflect the layering of land and legality found in distinctions between public land, public reserves, private real estate, and scientific land. Delaney (2010, 45) describes the practice of considering law's relationship to everyday life in terms of legal consciousness, as "legal consciousness is (and legal imaginaries are) often deeply inextricable from and informed by *spatial* consciousness (and spatial imaginaries)." For example, since the eruption of 2018, questions arise surrounding the future occupancy of Lava Zone 1, such as should Leilani become a national park or remain as a privately owned residential subdivision despite

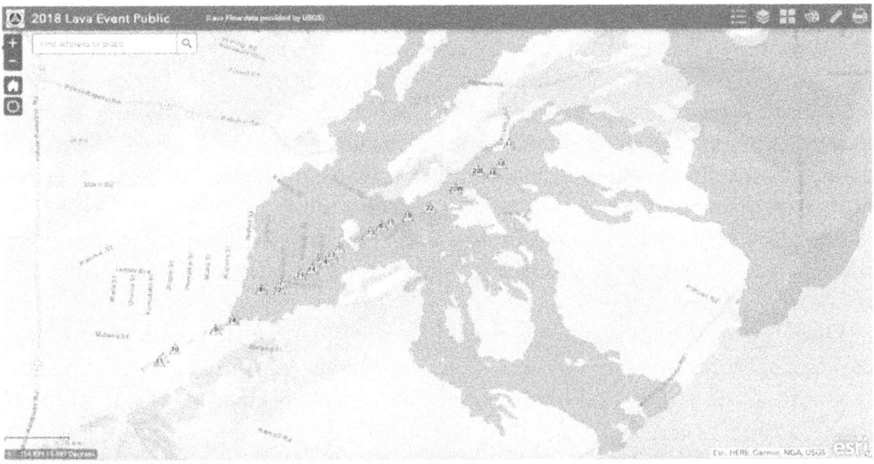

Figure 4.6 Fissure map.

County of Hawai'i Civil Defense website (with fissures as green triangles): https://hawaiicountygis.maps.arcgis.com/apps/webappviewer/index.html?id=3428cd9282ff431c865eb32761793078; Accessed Feb. 18, 2020)

the risk. Furthermore, the territorial nature of law over terrain can harness the localized framing of knowledge about terrain in terms of the formal naming of the most active of the 24 fissures from the 2018 Leilani eruption, as Figure 4.6 shows us. Moreover, that which is happening outside the national park in private backyards (as well as front yards) is a spectacle of nature, but also a spectacle of jurisdiction that is unfolding as this book is being written. Just as the thickness of the lava was mapped in Figure 4.5, the thickening of time, place, and law is evolving within the remaining subdivision of Leilani Estates as residents angrily call for the privatization of their publicly maintained streets from the onslaught of curious onlookers. What then is the role of the state in protecting natural phenomenon amidst the rights to private property? This question and this scenario revisits those same issues critically engaged with the creation of the HVNP through the colonial landscape of the United States in the 1900s, as discussed in chapter two.

Layering of land and legality

Jurisdiction, a concept of framing place through authority and order, is itself a fluid concept of spatio-temporality that reflects the evolving contextualized relationship between place and law, or as Dorsett and McVeigh (2012, 5) note, "jurisdictional thought and practice provides the visible (and occasionally invisible) forms that law takes." The term used by law to determine this relationship in the kinetic environment is a subjective term that positions law to be in charge, even when it's ultimately subject to the whims of a nature. Legal authority of the capricious naturally dynamic landscape is at best, fleeting and compelled to respond rather than direct or command. In this way, law's management over nature in motion is an illusory performance in which order and command camouflage the chaos and hazard of emergency, either sudden or slow-moving. Ironically, law itself can become a disaster in which no one wins and there are many losers. Lava Zone One is one such legal disaster, a slow-moving emergency in which law's control over nature is muted in the face of suddenly strong earthquakes, flowing lava and burning homes.

Disasters can happen in two ways. Either they can be predicted or they can be interpreted after the fact. Disasters in the making may be different (volcanic flows from shield volcanoes) than ongoing disasters (glacial melting), sudden disasters (sinkholes, tsunamis), or even unpredictable disasters (floods, earthquakes, explosive volcanic events from strato-volcanoes). Often, it's the slow-moving emergency that becomes an expected, if not normalized, disaster. In terms of law's response, the legal framework of disasters involves the diagnosis of the disaster, the legal response to the disaster, the legal interpretation of the disaster, and the forecasted prediction of the disaster. Yet, not all natural events, such as those described above, are disasters. In fact, the framing of kineticism in the nature environment by law through the terminology of disaster suggests the paternalistic justification of law's involvement, if not positioned centrality. Framing the movement of the dynamic landscape as "disaster" seems to convey language describing what otherwise would be natural, in terms of law's involvement to remedy the chaos of the situation. Mapping is one such governing technique to quell the anxiety of a landscape in motion

Governance in the form of lava zone mapping and response to eruption and lava flow illustrates law's mapping prowess to show, through heterotemporality of time and place, a thickness of order and stability through the static image. Through these maps of the static image even as the mapped image changes, law reveals the ability to conflate the present with the future while also accounting for the past, even while releasing itself from any financial liability through disclaimer. We know that time happens according to the earth's geologic clock, which either oozes, speeds up, or shoots into the sky often without pronouncement or regularity (with the possible exception of some geysers). Time also happens according to the human clock involving years, months, and days. As the most recent (and current) eruption of Kīlauea was ongoing from 1983 until 2018, the chronology of events and legal responses shaped by those events can be mapped as part of the discourse of territoriality and effectiveness of law's response to the potential chaos. Evident in the flow of the lavascape, law itself can be mapped according to its responses and reactions which are fluid in nature and transpire in myriad ways. As motile agent, lava on the move ultimately dictates the tone for law's ability to govern and respond to locally responsive cultural frameworks of order, authority, and resistance. Resistance to law's whims may even be as consistently reliable as the resistance of lava to barriers erected to contain the flow. Even evident through the tampering with lava, curfews restricting access to its flow, or calls to bomb lava on the move, law's turf is governed by nature. Yet, one might ask, when does Tutu Pele ever not have the right of way? When does lava obey the law? *Never*. And, when does the law obey lava? *Always*. As one resident notes, "Lava is not like other disasters….Madame Pele glories in tantalizing unknowables that terrorize our decision-making" (as qtd. in Serafin 2014).

Law is visualized through physical boundaries (fences, gates, roads) but also through the mapping of terrain. As the previous section shows, maps are a source of legal regulation insofar as the territory of law predicts movement and usage of land based upon mapped terrains. The mapping of the lavascape is further premised upon social and cultural forms of usage and presence. Temporality, terrain, and spectacle affect the mapping of land and the dynamic representation of land over time. Maps are law's attempt to regulate change and manage predictability, particularly in volatile landscapes. Yet, even as maps are visual representations of attempted order, maps are the material expression of law's turf as that which can be mapped can be understood and managed. Because of the changing scope of maps in dynamic landscapes, the management of the kinetic environment is a layered approach to land and legality. Through the legal materiality of lava and the recurrence of flows over roads, the literal layering of land and lava generates a fluid understanding of jurisdiction as a response to kineticism in the landscape. The terrain of that movement engenders and sustains evolving borderlands determined by the public quality of hazard and the territorializing of regulation.

As the stages of movement at Kīlauea change, so too does the landscape. When active, the lava can be molten and flowing, as in the recent Leilani flows. In 2018, a river of lava flowed from vents to ocean. Once the molten rock came into contact with the cold seawater, vast steam clouds formed and even a volcanically charged weather system ensued. In this stage, lava is physically untouchable and a spectacle independent from human management tactics. Free to move in and out of law's jurisdictional boundaries set by the national park or ignoring private property boundaries of homeowners, active lava clearly demonstrates its own kinetic agency to set the rules of movement with law relegated to the sidelines simply to observe and respond. We are witness to similar acts of engaged kineticism that transpire in non-volcanic environments including landscapes changed through the persistence of earthquakes, tsunamis, mudflows, landslides, raging rivers, flashfloods, and storm surges from hurricanes. Law can only watch as nature actively engages the terrain and changes the landscape. Similarly, the cooling of the lavascape renders new land as the legal materiality of property to which law responds.

The cycle of lava (molten, cooled, and hardened) is based upon the materiality of lava is its own agent creating the ebbs and flows of terrain. The entire Hawaiian archipelago is slowly corroding over time, with the once molten land succumbing to the ocean. However, once the landscape settles down, the stage of movement shifts from active to settled. At Kīlauea, the settled landscape is the cooling of lava. Cooled lava is hardened rock that perpetuates the illusion of a stable, firm earth that is done moving, if only for a while. Because geologic time is much lengthier than human time, and periods of settled lava may take place over many lifetimes. But, not always. On Hawai'i Island, the recurrence of lava is a point of normalcy. Black rock, or hardened lava, is everywhere. Whether as unique and convenient landscaping, cinder for paving roads, or rocks for lava rock walls, cooled lava is foundation for the island's architecture, landscaping, and cultural identity. However, the hardened lava rock landscape can be an illusion of stability as lava rock crumbles over time and at the seaside, can break off into the ocean in large chunks of land (cooled lava) known as lava delta collapses. With the evolving materiality of lava in mind, the illusion of lava is similar to the illusion of law in the kinetic terrain, as an enlivened force that crumbles when ignored or when its nonlegal foundations don't support legal response. Lava is a legal metaphor for a layered performance that looks to be solid and charge, until it's not. Lava Zone One and the repaving of the Chain of Craters Road are examples of legal metaphor that expose the illusory presence of law in the kinetic environment of the slow-moving, yet expected emergency of lava inundation.

The concept of law is visible in the legal metaphor. The Lava Zone Map is a legal metaphor of law as suggestion, just as the Lava Zone Map is made available for "general information and planning by land-use managers… there is no legislation requiring its use. The USGS provides hazard information but cannot advocate for, or require, its usage for a specific purpose" (Hawaiian Volcano Observatory n.d.). In other words, the exchange of private property in Lava Zone One is not prohibited by the Lava Zone Map, even if disclosed in real estate documents. Rather, just as law attempts to engender common sense, or as Valverde so nicely phrases it as "law's dream of a common knowledge" (Valverde 2003), the Lava Zone Map should be the educational foundation for common sense in living in an active lava flow area. Similarly, law cannot enforce common sense, but instead hopes to guide the public in the most sensible application of common sense, often a direction that is more paternalistically implemented than self-conclusory.

Similarly, as legal metaphor, we can look to the repaving of the Chain of Craters Road, a road within the HVNP that connects the lower sections of Puna. For the past "37 years of its 49 year existence," this road has been covered by lava and inaccessible to vehicular traffic (*Big Island Now* 2014). During the 2014 Pāhoa eruption, the Chain of Craters Road was needed as an emergency route for the nearly 9000 Puna residents whose primary

Figure 4.7 Lava covering pavement within the Hawai'i Volcanoes National Park. Photo credits: Phil Whitehouse, Creative Commons, Wikimedia.org. Accessed Feb. 18, 2020 at https://commons.wikimedia.org/wiki/Category:Chain_of_Craters_Road#/media/File:(Other)_End_of_the_road_(6480756615).jpg

road, Route 130, was threatened by lava. As a legal metaphor, the Chain of Craters road is similar to law as a constructed, yet malleable environment responsive to local conditions and needs. The road was a pedestrian walkway for years following its intersection by lava. Jurisdictionally, the road is layered as County of Hawai'i Mayor Billy Kenoi, U.S. Senator Brian Schatz, and National Park Superintendant Cindy Orlando agreed to its repaving despite overlapping boundaries to ensure its emergency usage in the 2014 Pāhoa eruption (Figure 4.7).

In conclusion, this chapter explores law's reaction to the unpredictability of the spectacle. As land is managed through national parks, the experience is managed in fleeting, unorganized ways. Law seeks to regulates the spectacle as an extension of legal territory through maps, prediction, and nonlegal actors. Perhaps paradoxically, law's ability to govern in kinetic environments is premised upon (and dependent upon) this relationship to nonlegal actors – science, culture, history, legend, and local indigeneity – for knowledge and validity. What this chapter shows is that law is not really law at all (if law is court order, a piece of legislation, a judicial opinion), but more of a general recognition (or attempted containment) of potential hazard/threat that must be acknowledged, managed, and framed as something in need of management. Examining the legal frameworks of movement in terms of risk, hazard, and predictability within the context of flowing lava illustrates that lava that is literally on the move as a material force that embodies the fluidity of law located in the accompanying assemblages of governance over this movement, namely maps, rules, and ad hoc jurisdictional authority. The dynamic lavascape is a spectacle of movement perpetuated by the durable legal phenomenon of molten lava. The ebbs and flow of this enlivened terrain provide texture to the lavascape, as it is sculpted by the whimsical directions of restless earth. The texture of the landscape includes human structures, such as residential neighborhoods, roads, and towns. This developed landscape pits law against nature in this anthropogenic wilderness. Yet, unlike the apparent stability of the landscape at Halema'uma'u Crater or the routinized eruptions of Strokkur Geysir, governing an active lava flow is much less straightforward and even, seemingly unmanageable. In this chapter, the semiotics of governance are tethered to the materiality of lava as a source of much legal drama. As lava flows, law attempts to intervene and manage the moving terrain by asserting jurisdiction over where the lava flows, who has access to the flow, and how the flow is perceived (as natural wonder or public threat). Despite the ostensibly obvious power of Tutu Pele to ultimately exercise her right of way, law seeks to triumph over nature in making the dynamic landscape of flowing lava a turf of its own.

Chapter 5

Knowing the ropes

As visible in Figure 5.1, the 1959 eruption of Kīlauea Iki within the Hawai'i Volcanoes National Park (HVNP) was a site to behold, even just to sit and watch the fountaining of lava from Kīlauea's caldera. The fluidity of lava during this particular eruption was similar to the fluid of water, just thicker and slower. Similar to the fountaining of Strokkur Geyser, the eruption of Kīlauea Iki bubbled forth from the earth. While the violence of the eruption lasted much longer than the quick-timed Strokkur, the two are linked through the expression of liquid elements from the earth, as molten rock or as superheated water. Yet despite the danger of being so close to this eruption, the close proximity of viewing distance between the eruption and the spectator generates understanding into the relationship between risk and common sense in the dynamic landscape. At the lavascape, the semiotics of risk offset and sometimes challenge the semiotics of common sense within the same setting. Judgements made by either law or individuals about the terrain and the temporality of movement within the terrain position the act of sightseeing at the spectacle a fluid conflation of law's presence and law's reception by a visiting public. The context of this fluidity is based in law's presence in the localized place of knowledge and culture stemming from life in a kinetic environment. The role of distance in law and proximity to the natural spectacle reveals a heightened sense of law's attempted control over the fluidity of environment.

Legal semiotics of hazard

In the fifty years since the eruption of Kīlauea Iki, the viewing of eruptive activity within the national park creates even more of a distance between spectacle and spectator. As discussed in chapter two, the purpose of visiting a dark crater at night is to see the glow of an active volcano and to feel the thrill of seeing actual molten lava and the orange glow visible from the designated viewing area of the crater's rim at Kīlauea. Similarly, the thrill of seeing and physically being right next to boiling water shooting out of the earth seduces visitors to Strokkur Geyser. The sheer proximity of humans

Figure 5.1 The 1959 Kīlauea Iki volcano eruption.

Source: USGS Public Domain: https://prd-wret.s3.us-west-2.amazonaws.com/assets/palladium/production/s3fs-public/vhp_img3042.jpg

to the active spectacle carries an implicit understanding of risk that may seem less overt in some tourist designations than in others. Yet, the risk is real despite its framing. It is the framing of risk that reveals the positionality of law's overt ability to govern the spectator and the spectacle, or not.

Risk is an ontological assemblage of knowledge, experience, and limit. From Foucault (1991), we know that risk is a normalizing institution that is sustained through social discipline. Risk itself is constituted through the project of governing through common sense, as "risk is not a real state of things, but a value-laden way of thinking of them and dealing with them" (O'Malley 2004). The unknown is present in risk, as risk is a concept in which future action is preconceived as possible. Risk conveys the potential of harm. We see risk in a variety of ways. Risk becomes visible through signs, gates, official personnel, and even other people. Culture is a manager of risk through practices of social discipline. Conversely, risk constitutes culture, as common sense is culturally framed, determined, and enacted. The knowledge of risk is both conceptual and actual in terms of "knowing the ropes." "Knowing the ropes" is a framework of knowledge in which risk is accepted, even embraced. In kinetic environments, risk is a constant, a reality understood as common sense. Common sense is the normative framing of such knowledge, as an essentialized understanding of the threat of the unknown. Common sense is the self-interest that protects the individual from the dangers of the future unknown (Tyler 1990). For example, common sense in an enlivened landscape would suggest the molten lava is hot. Or, that water spurting from a geyser will burn. However, the relationship between law and common sense is one of reciprocation in which law frames the ontological basis of common sense while common sense steers law to act. Yet, conversely, law and common sense may be distinct from one another, as common sense may not actually depend on law to foster or manage what people already know. Law may be attempting to foster a generalized common sense that otherwise would be absent from different cultures and ways of living. We know that common sense can be tyrannical in its attempt to normalize instinct and response to threat. Law seems to project the same desire for normalization in thought and response. If common sense protects the individual, then who is law protecting? The state? The individual? The spectacle? This chapter considers the relationship of law to common sense by examining performances of jurisdiction at Kīlauea and Iceland's Strokkur Geyser that arise differently in creating a normative construction of risk and a legal culture of "knowing the ropes."

Through property management, or the seeming lack thereof, law has constructed its ownership over the natural spectacle through signs and warning of risk. Common sense balances law's role in seeking compliance to rules and regulations at the spectacle; however, common sense is neither common nor always sensical (Simon 2007). Seeing the glow from molten lava or waiting for a geyser to burst are experiences that law strives to manage through the management of common sense. Through the visual generation of viewing rules, viewing places, and creating (in)access to the spectacle, law assumes the semiotic governance of the human perspective in these wild terrains (Harvey 1996). At Iceland's Strokkur Geysir, the visibility of law is much less overt. Neither Icelandic national park or national land reserve, Strokkur Geysir is open and accessible to the public who can access the spectacle from the cafeteria and giftshop across the street. At the entry point, law merely appears as a list of suggestions for optimal geyser viewing posted at an unmanned gate.

However, at the HVNP, law's presence is much more materially present. From signs to constructed landscapes that designate public space for human presence at the spectacle, the Park has, from its inception, served as manager for this enlivened volcanic landscape. As manager, the Park has paved roads, constructed vistas, and a gated Kīlauea Volcano. The signs of law are present through signage, fences, gates, and figures of patrolling rangers. Whether for purposes of public safety or environmental preservation, law's presence at the volcano and the geyser shape our viewing of the kinetic spectacle. The resulting *lavascape* (Marusek 2019) is a negotiation between law, nature, and the visiting public that positions the kineticism of nature as a turf that law must materially operationalize for public safety. Through visual markings, regulatory messaging, and often its own distancing, law reveals itself as a spectacle of performative (and illusory) governance that is mediated by competing understandings of common sense.

What is common about common sense? In the dynamic landscape, common sense is sensory, embodied, visual, and hermeneutic of hegemony. What might be uncommon about common sense? If culturally determined, common sense would be contextually framed and specific to the knowledge of the ropes from a particular spectacle. For example, the timing of the geyser or the likelihood of eruption can be found in tourist literature that seeks to educate the visitor about local knowledge. Knowing the ropes can be read in a guide to the spectacle, but also experienced through life at the spectacle with or without the guiding hand of law. Law is limited in its dictation of common sense as not every possible scenario can be conceived of in advance, as the visitor is as dynamic as the landscape s/he is visiting.

As the legal semiotics promoting common sense, the negotiation of risk and hazard at Kīlauea and Strokkur becomes visible through the semiotic of law represented by the sign. Signs can be placards on poles that provide notification of hours, temperature, and other such measurables that temper what common sense construes and sees. Similarly, hiking signs and ropes remind the visitor that the spectacle is wild and that law creates a protective barrier for both the visitor and the spectacle alike. The semiotics of governing risk can be as simple as a roped-off space, but as complex as the synesthetic embodiment of governance with spectacle. Sensorially, the audibility of radio warnings about volcanic eruption, the sight of an ash plume, the odor of volcanic emissions containing sulfur dioxide (also known as vog), and the heated spray of water at the edge of the safety zone at the geyser inform the visitor of the living spectacle (Marusek 2017; Philippopoulos-Mihalopoulos 2013). The presence of law is visual in scope insofar as the uniforms of the National Guard, the National Park rangers, those of Civil Defense, and the police visibly distinguish law from nature even as the nature of law is the presence of the uniform. The vehicles of law, such as the National Guard's Humvee, the police's blue light, the ranger's jeep, even the white trucks of Hawai'i County Civil Defense remind the onlooker of law's presence in guarding the spectacle as well as managing the other unknown, the visiting public.

Vehicular presence in Iceland, however, is less authoritarian in scope as at Kīlauea. In Iceland, vehicular remnants in the dynamic landscape are an intrusion, an undelible marking of the past on future generations. For example, tire tracks in peat that have veered off the pavement (off-roading) are seen as a travesty insofar as the environment is itself scarred.[1] Such errant driving is an aspect of common sense that errs in judgement and exhibits the extension of unregulated tourism in Iceland. Yet, driving on a glacier by tourist-laden pickup trucks with giant inflated rubber tires is a normative thing to so. The difference between the driving off road on soil and driving off road on the glacier is that the glacier, as ice, is impervious to vehicular scarring by tire tracks. The glacier wins and endures as a solid sheet of ice, impervious to human destruction. Therefore, in Iceland, common sense would dictate that driving on a glacier is preferable to driving off the paved asphalt for the reason that ice doesn't memorialize tire tracks the same way that peat does. And, contrary to American-based common sense, the spectacle of nature does not always need law to protect it. Common sense is both culturally normative and hegemonic in its approach to managing human presence in the kinetic environment.

The legal environment is one of accessibility and spectacle. However, the liability of the park, the State of Hawai'i, or the federal government, is invoked despite the premise of a wild nature preserve, as stated in the purpose of the national park to govern a site of wild land for public use. In this way, the public land as well as public land are managed for their own good. The public may be perceived as needing instruction, while the land can remain wild if it is, ironically, managed by law. For those visitors who fall into Kīlauea Caldera (Stack 2019) or those visitors who do not heed the law's instruction at Strokkur Geyser and get burned, the law can only be at fault if it is inattentive to the spectacle. Because the visitor at the spectacle is herself wild, in the sense of possible unrestraint or demonstrated disregard for law's presence at the spectacle, law is both positioned as responsible but also without blame in lieu of absent common sense.

Spectators at the volcano are seemingly protected by law, but are they? Are they rather governed by their own sense of hazard and danger even when the signs are not in view? What then is the relationship between governing semiotics and their implementation through common sense? At Kīlauea, the presence and accessibility of the visiting public are managed by law in order for purposes of public safety first and protection of the environment second. Except in Iceland, the converse situation arises, where the legal protection of the environment takes precedence over the legal protection of those visitors to the spectacle who do not exhibit their own individual understandings of common sense.[2] Common sense is therefore anything but common.

Containing the lava: regulating eruption

When the lava is wild, the law steps into action in ways to directly alter the progress of eruption. During the 1973 eruption of Eldfell on the Icelandic Island of Heimaey, water cannons were used to pump seawater against the flowing lava in an effort to cool the molten rock (Einarsson 1974). By using nature against nature, law succeeded in drowning the lava to halt the molten flow. In Hawai'i, other approaches have been considered but much less successful. Diverting Kīlauea's lava into channels with bulldozers has been attempted (Hajek 2014) as has the construction of a berm around private property by a concerned homeowner Kīlauea (Lincoln 2014). Additionally, a bridge over the lava was proposed (*Hawaii News Now* 2018), as were walls to contain the lava (MacDonald 1962). Even bombs were detonated to stop lava flows on Mauna Loa in 1935 and 1942 by the U.S. Air Force (Lockwood and Torgerson 1980) but with no success. Subsequent aerial bombing on Mauna Loa occurred in 1975 and 1975 on prehistoric flows to test the viability of using bombs to stop future flows. A total of 36 bombs were dropped and determined to be an effective method of lava diversion (Lockwood and Torgerson 1980).

Through the bombing, law attempted to (literally) arrest the spectacle. Yet, even as bombing the lava was determined ineffective and only coincidental to the stoppage of the flow (Hawaiian Volcano Observatory 2017), attempts to criminalize the spectacle have shifted from the terrain itself to the visitation of the terrain. Criminalizing the unsanctioned sightseeing of the spectacle is the modern approach of law to regulate the effects of eruption through fining unpermitted lava tours, maintaining curfews enforced by the National Guard, staging roadblocks, and creating the trope of the "lava loiter," or persons who photographed the Leilani flow behind the blockades set up by the state and enforced by the military (Wu 2018). Yet, law does not act alone, as "any hazard mitigation effort [by law] must be looked at in terms of its total cultural, social, and economy impact" (*Big Island Video News* 2014).

In response to the 2014 Pāhoa flow, two brothers from Pāhoa, Brady and Myke Metcalf, designed a t-shirt that depicted a wave of lava with Tutu Pele surfing with her arms outstretched underneath the words "2014 Go With the Flow Tour" (Associated Press 2014). This was an image of Pele doing what she does best, creating flowing lava. From the town's perspective, as depicted in the image of Pele surfing, Pāhoa was a stop on her 2014 Tour.

The personification of the lava was also evident in a 2016 headline of the local newspaper, *Hawaii Tribune-Herald* (September 18, 2016), "The Plume Is Not Your Friend." This headline was intended to emphasize the dangers of visiting the "billowy white 'laze' plume" that looked like a puffy white cloud where the lava entered the ocean, but was actually "condensed seawater steam laced with hydrochloric acid and tiny shards of volcanic glass," as written in the article. In an attempt to curb risky ocean-based visitation trying to see the lava entry point into the sea, the headline tries to redirect the practice of common sense. The realization that recently erupted lava from the Leilani flow may still pose a threat can be read as governable common sense in Hawai'i County Mayor Harry Kim's October 30, 2018, Fifth Supplementary Emergency Proclamation:

> WHEREAS, the USGS HVO has identified many hazards when traversing over lava flow fields, including subsurface residual molten lava and gases that may not be visible; due to the hazards involved, the USGS HVO and Hawai'i County Civil Defense Agency have noted that injuries while traversing over lava flow fields are common and deaths have occurred.
>
> Taming the wild landscape, law as manager of risk in a setting of enlivened nature. Through the failed attempts of lava to be controlled by legal mandate (bombs, pronouncements), we can see that legal positivism is indeed limited in its ability as the foundation for governing. As common sense and risk are culturally constituted, law is limited in its temporary restrictions of communities inundated by lava, evident in the rebuilding of homes on properties covered by lava throughout Puna. People rebuild despite the risk.

Teasing the spectacle

The many dimensions of common sense provide a way to consider the human response to the unknown thrills of the kinetic environment. Generating the thrill, often going outside the reaches of law in these environments, serves as the catalyst for engaging in risk. In this sense, common sense and the consequences of risk are extended to "own" the associated hazard of the risk. No longer is the law seemingly fully in charge of the range of possibilities in such enlivened terrains. Law's imagination of controlling behavior is limited in what is ultimately nature's jurisdiction, the landscape in motion. Through the thrill-seeking actions of those who seek to play with nature, law itself is tested. The consequential act of challenging this otherwise normative hegemonic legal understanding of the spectacle as dangerous and off-limits leads to a sense of playing with the legal imagination in nature's jurisdiction. Because law has a difficult time in controlling nature in the dynamic landscape, the common-ness of common sense supporting law's imagination of control is tested as the risk itself is tested. Law's perspective on risk in these kinetic environments is a conservative performance in the normativity of common sense and ensuing risk. Playing with nature is redefining and re-performing common sense in spite of law's guidance. Such play is often an affront to law's position of authority over the natural, as this section of the chapter will demonstrate through examples that tease the spectacle. In other words, the risk and hazard of the spectacle, as framed by law, is tested by thrill-seekers who, in playing with nature, also play with the law, testing the common sense approach taken by law in managing the spectacle.

Just as the spectacle constantly changes and evolves within a state of fluidity, the dynamic landscape of Kīlauea challenges the stability of law's turf. Just as the cycles of land range from molten to cooled, from sacred land to landscaping cinder or even the basis for local asphalt for paving roads, the ebbs and flow of terrain position nature as its own agent. As Tutu Pele moves where she wants, lava oozes through towns in a culturally interpreted effort to "clean house" (Jonsson 2014). Pele is on the move, as the jurisdiction of the volcano is dynamically understood with local residents riding the wave of Pele's activities. She even generates her own weather in a phenomenon characterizing actively volcanic environments. All of this motility presents a challenge to the static quality of what would be considered law's authority in the natural terrain. Nature's practice of jurisdiction (Ford 2001) keeps law guessing. In response, law tries to assume the upper hand of nature. One example of this would be the creation of the HVNP, as discussed in chapter two. Another would be the bombing of the Mauna Loa flow in the 1930s. This particular attempt to arrest nature, literally, by bombing the flow of lava, proved inconclusive. Although the bombing demonstrated law's might, scientists at the time argued that the stopping of the flow was purely coincidental. The legacy of law's attempted prowess of the 1930s against the lava continues to pervade Hawai'i Island, as undetonated bombs have been found in the open lava fields as recently as March 2020 (Katz 2020). During the Pahoa eruption in 2014 and the Leilani eruption of 2018, law respected the movement of the lava by allowing it to move over the land without attempted restrictions such as bombs or berms. Nonetheless, law did manage one triumph over the dynamic landscape in Iceland in 1973 at Heimaey when cannons pumping sea water on the lava flow actually did stop the path of molten lava (Einarsson 1974). The tension between law's command and those who resist results often in harm, or even death (Whittlesey 2014), but importantly *not always*.

In this chapter, legal discourse would suggest ownership and control over nature at the hands of those who wish to play with nature. Playing with nature in the context of the dynamic landscape would include the human interaction with an enlivened nature, or a nature that is oozing, erupting, or boiling hot. Playing with nature is playing with jurisdiction (Brigham 2009). Yet, jurisdiction over the natural environment in national parks or other sites of spectacle is a manmade construction evident in the semiotics of national parks, reserve areas, and other governmental forms of claim to the land. Governance at the kinetic environment attempts to dictate who can either access or simply play with nature. In this way, jurisdiction is culturally determined, as the differences between Kīlauea and Iceland show. Law at these places is constituted by local cultural understandings of present and future risks, insofar as playing with nature is a contradictory act between perceptions of harming nature or lived realities of harnessing nature for human benefit. Indeed, semiotics of jurisdiction challenge understandings of power that perpetuate a schism between man over environment or environment over man in accordance with perceived legal authority in places and cultural activities involving risk.

Risk to the person is often embraced for a variety of reasons ranging from pleasure to curiosity to individual gain. Law's authority over nature is a limited jurisdiction, as demonstrated in the following cases that involve the socio-semiotics of challenging law's authority over nature. Such challenges not only respond to jurisdictional purview, but also to the normative discourse that in terms of nature, that law (and man) should be in charge in the first place. The normative discourse that law controls nature is itself challenged through the actions taken in the following events. Holistically, this chapter examines the legal discourse of control as it is invoked and challenged in events that play with nature and concurrently, play with law's jurisdiction over nature. Semiotically, law cannot always be in control and the consequences of appearing out of control beckon law to clamp down on those who play. Law is worried that it will be blamed, as again, in the normative discourse, law is in charge and able to mitigate harm to a man from nature. However, the socio-semiotic that is generated from events that challenge this discursive position in reimagining law's role in nature (Stone 2010). Is law really in charge of nature? Who essentially is in charge of human interactions with nature? Anthoropogenically, it might be argued that nature stands to be harmed by man. However, in the context of geothermal energy, it is conversely the opposite, namely that man stands to be harmed by a boiling hot molten landscape that ultimately is fully beyond his control. Playing with nature in this context is the same as playing with risk and risk is an individual act that transcend legalized formal judgement by not asking permission but just doing. Rather than reactions of criminality, perhaps the law could reimagine, or reconstruct itself as the onlooker rather than the responsible party. Such a repositioning would allow law and man to engage with nature on individual terms, particularly in those environments in which law is clearly not able to fully be in control due to the whims of a dynamic landscape.

Teasing the spectacle is a way for spectators to transcend law's governance attempt and to embrace, if not experiment directly with the spectacle, and most importantly, to challenge the normative presumption that we need law to manage the spectacle in the name of risk, hazard and common sense. The following examples demonstrate that law not only does not own the spectacle, but does not own the only approach to the spectacle. In this way, teasing the spectacle is a way to keep the spectacle public through direct engagement. These approaches to playing with nature are also playing with law's imagination of complete jurisdiction over the kineticism of the environment.

Teasing the volcanic spectacle happens in a variety of fun, creative ways. At Strokkur, in an effort to create "'landscape art'," Chilean artist Marco Evaristti dumped five liters of red food coloring into the geyser (*Iceland Monitor* 2016). Acquitted of criminal charges by the Icelandic courts, the artist succeeded in capturing the spectacle in a striking photograph of pinkish, purplish water erupting against a backdrop of blue sky and brown ice. At Kilauea, two local residents dipped an egg beater and some golf clubs in the 2014 Pāhoa flow and upon photographing themselves in the act, were arrested and later found guilty of second-degree criminal trespass. One of the residents, Ruth Crawford, said of the 2100-degree lava, "It was very hot and I felt like my face was burning. It was really hot" (Associated Press and Klausner 2014). Capturing the heat at the spectacle however can be done in more harnessed ways however. Whether as cooking over geothermal heat in Iceland over specially fashioned ovens alongside the roadway in villages and towns, or cooking marshmallows over the heat of a subdued lava flow under the moonlight, the volcanic spectacle teases common sense through perceived (and accepted) risk. Law is not always present, despite that the notion that "law is all over" (Sarat) as the temporality of risk is weighed against the temporality of law as evident in the photograph of golfers continuing their shot despite the ash cloud rising 20,000 feet into the sky behind them at a golf course less than a mile from the erupting Kīlauea in May 2018 (Cunningham 2018).

Negotiations of common sense

The rules of the game that law tries to win against the thrill-seeker at the spectacle, as noted above, are not always the same. Sometimes law's presence is less overtly 'law like' through normative regulations and policing presence, and more subtly evoked through knowledge and self-interest. In terms of punishing those who challenge law's authority at the spectacle, we can change the rules to ask, does law always need to win? Does law really want to win or does it just want to assume a façade of being in control over man as well as nature? Is law really just a façade? At Iceland's geyserscape, the appearance of law is much more subtle in conveying the risk and potential of the hazard from the spectacle through the common sense associated with self-care and self-interest in the protection against harm.

The rawness of nature's fluidity can also be witnessed as a spectacle of water shooting out of the earth. At Iceland's Strokkur Geysir, the public has twenty-four hour, open, unrestricted access to an active volcanic geyser that erupts every 8–10 minutes. The presence of law is minimal at this site, represented as a gate (that is open and unmanned), as ropes roughly mid-calf in height that create a boundary for a walkway, and small signs along the way that warn of the water's likely temperature (Figure 5.2a and b). Additionally, there is a sign at the gate that welcomes visitors while warning of the possible hazards at this site (Figure 5.3). Unlike the distance created

Figure 5.2a Sign on the rope displaying the temperature of the water.

Source: Author

Figure 5.2b Strokkur Geyser. (Circle indicates position of sign in Figure 5.2a)

Source: Author

between the overlook and the volcanic glow at Halema'uma'u Crater, the public can walk right up to (and in, if desired) the geyser. The geyser is located a short walk from a parking lot of a hotel and cafeteria on the other side of the two-lane highway. It is unclear if the geyser is under the ownership of the Icelandic government or in the private hands of the adjacent tourist spot. Yet regardless of the ownership (or ensuing jurisdiction), the site is particularly under-constructed. Nature here is unspoiled by law's presence

Figure 5.3 Warnings at Strokkur.

Source: Author

as the public are afforded easy (and free) access. Access has not been privatized either as in the model of an American national park or from the tourist destination immediately on the other side of the road. Risk has been individualized to be the pronounced responsibility of the onlooker through the sign that prescribes care, respect, visitation only, extreme caution, and common sense. In particular, the consequences for ignoring such mandates will result in harm. This harm is framed through a visitor's stupidity, or lack of common sense, rather than the geyser itself as dangerous. This nuance is articulated in the sign's language: *Don't test the temperature with your hands, it will burn*; *The nearest hospital is 62 km away*; *Remember that the water is 80–90 degrees C (176–194 degrees F) is will burn badly*. Interestingly, the language of the sign is in the global language of tourism (English), even with temperature conversions in Fahrenheit. The presence of English seems to transcend local cultural engagement with the geyser, that might be written in Icelandic.

When juxtaposing the lavascape of Halema'uma'u with the geyserscape of Strokkur, the distance between onlooker and the spectacle itself illustrates competing perspectives about law's role in public safety when visiting active volcanic spectacles. Risk is framed at Strokkur as the individualized responsibility of the public, rather than that of the government/national park, to be responsible for their own safety. In comparison, the temperature of the lava is not posted at the crater's rim for visitors, and the crater itself is closed to visitors, unless of course they fall in by accident. Ironically, risk may be a point of attraction in visiting Strokkur. Just as seeing lava glow in the distance and hearing rocks tumbling into the molten abyss, seeing water shoot out of the earth from geysers and being close enough to feel the earth shake and feel the spray of heated water is an experience that must happen in person. Danger that is tangible and real enables the onlooker to realize and embrace the risk, which in turn heightens the experience of spectacle. At Strokkur, if caution is not exercised, visitors may inadvertently stand right on top of the geyser's vent before running to safety when the water shoots forth, if attention is not heeded to the sign that states *Never stand on the edges or close to the hot springs.*[3] The law cannot shoulder the blame for the hazard if the commonsensical approach to risk (i.e. to read the signs) is ignored.

In conclusion, at both the geyser and the crater's rim, law is clearly distinct from courts or lawyers: law that is personified through rangers or represented by signs, displays, barriers such as lavarock walls, ropes, or even an opened gate, is dependent upon the reception of the message conveyed by the visiting public. Sometimes that message is direct, such as at the crater's rim and threatens with legal import (Figure 5.4). Other times, such as at

Figure 5.4 Sign at Devastation Hiking Trail on crater's rim within the HVNP with enlarged detail.

Source: Author

Strokkur, that message is determined though individual common sense and anticipated compliance. As indicated on this sign, the law is cited ("36CFR 1.5 (a)(1)") and declares the punishment if violated ("Violators Subject to Fine"). An example of this knowing can be seen in these signs above, from a trail in the HVNP. This trail is at a place in which the volcanic wind from the volcano flows. This wind can be unpredictable in its carrying of noxious fumes. At the head of the trail, in a wooded area, this sign has been erected to warn of the dangers of accessing this part of the volcano. Is there a right to access even for those who choose not to exercise their own common sense? Who controls this right? Should individual risk take second place to institutional framing of risk? The sign issued by the U.S. Department of the Interior, the federal agency responsible for the national park system, fails to allow for an individualized practice of common sense that might take the visitor beyond the sign's boundaries. Is the lack of common sense a crime, or is common sense subject itself to a colonizing force that normalizes normative behavior? Law regulates through a variety of methods, from the building of roads to the mapping of hazard-prone areas. Law's method for regulating change and natural spectacle is organized as government agencies that diagnose and seek solutions to changing terrain. However, in landscapes that are kinetically premised upon motion and movement, legal authority arising from organizations often competes with individual common sense. Law ironically hopes we will use our own best judgment, but doesn't seem to fully trust us to make the best choice as arrests, punishment, and blocked access to sites of spectacle occur. Paradoxically, movement and materiality in mobile places challenge law's normative governing capacity in fleeting moments whether in public parks, on private land, or standing near a stream of oozing molten lava.

At Halema'uma'u, the spectacle is managed in a passive, restrained manner as the distancing of the crater is tethered to the descriptive displays discussing the eruptive history and possibility. At the HVNP, safety is conveyed through distance. Rangers, as the Park's law-enforcement personnel under federal jurisdiction, are actively present with law's physical boundaries evident through signs and walls. Yet, at Strokkur, there are no rangers and signs that embody law's presence do not threaten with legal sanction if violated. Law is present in both places through a presupposed dependency, or even the mere acknowledgment that there will be rules that govern the spectacle. These spectacles are both framed through rules that govern common sense. As Ian Hacking (2003, 22) writes, "No general theory about what determines a choice of risks can be offered, for too many contingent facts and local stories affect the choice."

Law's function at the spectacle is different at Strokkur than it is at Kīlauea. At Halema'uma'u, the law is pastoral with a purpose to protect and necessarily provide guidance for the visiting public. However, at Strokkur, the law is much less overt (there are no rangers), even absent as visitors are encouraged to draw upon their own common sense for how to act. The direction for safety are provided by the signs and reinforced through the rope boundaries or active rangers. Possible dangers are then up to the individual visitor to be aware of and take precaution against. Despite law's framing of these places as normative sites of jurisdiction via the management of public safety in unstable terrains, the regulation of these sites is ultimately a reflection of local culture. Such rules and frameworks for access to these places are locally and culturally determined and reflect a particular society's approach to law as the source of regulation. Often, it is not the government's job to protect the individual but instead becomes the individual visitor's imperative to assume responsibility to protect herself by exercising common sense and employing the necessary protections against burns, falls, or other dangers associated with nature. Yet, law at the lavascape is arguably contrasted by law at the geyserscape. In Hawai'i, Kīlauea Volcano is the amalgamation of Western science and Hawaiian indigeneity, which supports harmonious relations between geological surveys and cultural beliefs viewing the volcano as home to Pele, the Hawaiian Goddess of Fire. In Iceland, nature is protected against human's intrusion, evident in damages that will affect future generations.

Returning to the relationship of lava and geothermal activity to law, we can examine the cases of Hawai'i and Iceland to consider the jurisdictional fallacies that stem from the idea of managing nature through regulation that become evident in these dynamic landscapes. The subsequent jurisprudential contributions of land management in these areas of risk reflect the larger discourse concerning the relationship of law and place. Such jurisdictional fallacies include the management of risk, the framing of public space, and the temporal considerations inherent to legal jurisdictional framing of natural spectacle. If the dynamic landscape is itself a legal metaphor, then law in these public places of natural phenomena provides a flexible, fluid, and non-normative insight into the purposes of regulation in the larger discourse of governance over nature. As Steinberg (1995) notes, "property law is yet another tool for imposing order on the chaos of nature." Property, as John Brigham (1990) describes, is a legal construction that transcends materiality. As "the relationship between people and the thing," the "social function of property" (Karl Renner as cited by Brigham (1990)) acts as "governing relations among people" (Vandevelde as cited in Brigham (1990), pp. 3, 20). The social function of public property through the creation of national parks is to preserve nature for present and future public benefit. In this way, the preservation of nature is intended to memorialize the past, protect in the present, and conserve for the future. Ironically, environments in such places are less "natural" and more "owned and regulated" by governments for land usage and property management. The management of these places is similar to the regulation of zoos (Braverman 2012) as wild elements (be they animals or landscapes) are contained, tamed, and controlled through regulatory measures. However, these environments themselves remain wild via such phenomenon as glacial melting, wildfire, drought, flood, and similar climatic events. Law's response to dynamic natural changes in preserved settings must be one of evolving attentiveness, particularly when considering individualized common sense and indigenous perspectives on their reserve.

Notes

1 In March 2016, I spoke at length with two members from the Department of Integration at the Umhverfisstofnun, Environment Agency of Iceland in Reykjavik, who shared their perspectives about lava, law, and tourism in Iceland with me.
2 In March 2016, I interviewed a faculty member in the Department of Law at the University of Iceland in Reykjavik, who shared her ideas with me about tourism and law in Iceland.
3 As happened to me when visiting Strokkur in March 2016.

Concluding remarks: jurisprudence of the enlivened terrain

This book is about the life of law on an active volcano. More specifically, the book sees life on an active volcano in the middle of the ocean as legal metaphor. Here, lava is like law in that both operate in predictable, yet spontaneous ways. While the volcano endures, law is something newer. Western-based jurisprudence, focused on ownership and control, operates almost in contrast to the steady stream of either lava or steam found in these places. Law's forced hand of reaction happens in response to the volcano's activity. The volcano is a spectacle, and similarly, so is law in the volcanic environments of Hawaii Island firstly, and Iceland, secondly. The eruptive nature of volcanoes results in flowing lava whether above the earth's crust or beneath it in heated waters. This movement of molten rock results in a dynamic landscape, or kinetic environment, in which the landscape is on the move and ever-changing. The stability associated with law's ability to provide social foundations becomes a spectacle when nature confronts law. This confrontation leads to law as a spectacle in which eruption, unseen currents, but also prediction, share understandings of how life happens in ways that cause this foundation to evolve and respond to nature. The materiality of the spectacle, whether molten (or cooled) lava or eruptive geothermal hotspots (geysers) seems to parallel the materiality of law insofar as legal materiality, often unseen in everyday banalities. However, just as social order is dynamic, so is nature. In the places where lava is a constant presence, law's ability to govern is called into question involving both human and natural influences.

If such local custom, or local knowledge about dynamic phenomena, is the case, then law is more how society operates rather than what happens in a courtroom. We experience law each time we turn on the tap, cross the street (crosswalk or jaywalking), or operate a motor vehicle. Law is dynamic in its forms and how it happens in fleeting, spontaneous, unplanned, and taken-for-granted ways. Perhaps the rigidity of law is the perspective that law happens only in the courtroom and that the experience of law must involve either lawyers or judges. This could be termed a topographical perspective on law, in which the surface of legality is limited to certain predesignated places, such as courtrooms or police cars.

However, a more penetrative, less-topographical approach to law would involve the legality that arises when we take a more expansive perspective on what law is or how it happens. Like an erupting volcano, law is a spectacle that we experience in a variety of ways as the experience of law becomes a form of ownership over the process. Knowledge of the spectacle can be gained through repetitive experiencing and leads to the conclusion that legal experience is a form of capital, or a localized knowledge about how the system works.

The spectacle is the glow of molten lava or the sudden showering of water from a geyser illustrates the spectacle of law. Like lava, law has similar qualities of fluidity, materiality, temporality, and illusion as the dynamic landscape of Kīlauea and Strokker illustrate. The lavascape is a legal metaphor characterized through the epistemologies of jurisdiction, the legalization of the spectacle, the topologies of governance, and the negotiations of risk and common sense against the backdrop of hazard. The legal geography of the dynamic landscape illustrates the motion of law as performed chaos in an environment enlivened by science, culture, and history.

The movement of nature compels law to be present and responsive in a variety of ways. As a spectacle of modern legality that transforms place into lavascape, place enlivens law through its kinetic presence. Law responds with semiotic markers of its presence that construct a place as legally material. Boundaries are created as material expressions of ownership and management that epistemologically engender a sense of regulation. Consequentially, the resulting forms of legal regulation in these places sustain a model of governance for human relationships with nature. In these unstable volcanic environments, the legal materiality of a dynamic earth is evident through its movement, its bubbling, its eruption. Whether in the future or the here and now, the kineticism of the dynamic landscape is claimed and managed by law. The legality generated by contained as well as unrestricted dynamic landscapes further challenges American legal standards pertaining to risk management, land ownership, and jurisdiction as premised upon stable, unchanging terrain. Additionally, the spatio-temporality of a landscape in motion raises important questions about notions of legal reasoning that jurisprudentially shapes property discourse and relationships with the environment. The study of dynamic landscapes further contributes to larger questions involving the epistemology of property, regulation, and ownership in public environments. Specifically, the concept of the dynamic landscape, in conjunction with the semiotics of regulation that manage public spaces within the volcanic environments of flowing lava in Hawaii and geothermal bubbling in Iceland, characterizes the kineticism of the legal environment. Such semiotics of regulation include the jurisdictional creation of national parks that surround natural phenomena, the absence of formal boundaries in regions of natural phenomena, and structures that warn of spectacle-related risk (such as fences, boardwalks, and signs).

Modern legality is constitutive. It reflects as well as constructs an evolving society in which law permeates everyday activities and places. We can see law through its material presence, whether as metaphor semiotic directives found in signs and markers, or as the clear manifestation of jurisdiction, as evident in the construction of national parks. In each of these, regulation is the adaptation of law to place through presumptions of normativity and expected frameworks of usage. While law seems to understand that nature ultimately has the right of way, the fluid materiality of the dynamic landscape complicates normative conceptualizations of property and the public environment that rely upon static conceptualizations of place and expectation. But, what happens when moving lava stops? New land is formed. Often this new land, or accreted land, happens over pre-existing private land. The concomitant property narrative positions the state against the individual in the ownership of nature. Perhaps the private property seems arguably less stable than publicly owned lands; yet what can be owned is itself a fluid category. In the end, ownership of the kinetic environment is a display of law. Arguably, such a display is the performance of law as the ultimate authority over nature. Yet, nature is a dynamic force and through its own agency, the control of calamity is beyond law's reaches. This would lead to a jurisprudence of the here and now, as predictability of risk and the governance of hazard is an imperfect legal science. Law itself is the spectacle.

The book concludes with a jurisprudential analysis of movement associated with nature, social and cultural aspects of materiality, and the fluidity of law. Jurisprudentially, law is characteristic of a landscape in motion. Legality, as law's relationship with place, is performed in public places (such as national parks), private places (involving property ownership disputes), and in nature (the spectacle of lava or related natural phenomena). Law is constantly evolving and fluid, responsive to a variety of natural, social, and culture influences on landscapes in motion. The spectacle is really law, as law is really premised on fluidity (it changes, it morphs, it moves from legal to non-legal bases (science, culture, politics) and durability. Law can take many forms (law is fluid just like the movement of the environment that we see but can't fully see).

Like lava, law is a viscous substance that flows with the tides of normativity and oozes through boundaries it creates as jurisdiction. Understandings about the jurisdiction of law to land to the motile landscape position Western law as a newcomer in places with indigenous relationships to the dynamic landscape, as the continued reverence of the Native Hawaiian relationship to Kīlauea shows. Law seeps into the crevices of racist imperialism through land conquest and strategies to govern the dynamic landscape through legal positivist frameworks of land control represented through post-colonial drippings framing the contemporary national park setting. As the lava flows, the legal conceptualizations of property, ownership, and accessibility drift in the unsteady currents of assumed authority and control over the movement of the land. Like the hardening of lava, law, as a substance of authority, congeals when it seeks too much control over the uncontrollable.

As a material substance, lava can be molten, oozing, still, soft, hard, and crumbled. The materiality of law in the dynamic landscapes is made tangible through mapped textures of movement. The fabric of regulation is woven as legal responses to sightseeing, the affirmation of jurisdiction, and the management of common sense. As a thread that holds together this cloth of legal spectacle, perspectives on risk fray the edges of law's management over the public quality of the spectacle in the changing terrain.

Change, or kinetic shifts in the landscape, reflect the temporality of lava as well as of law. Through the stages of movement, lava temporally interrupts the stability of landscape and practices of property. Through the stages of movement in law, the temporality of its non-legal contributors surface. In reckoning with the changing terrain of the dynamic landscape, law relies upon scientific knowledge, cultural knowledge, and historical legacy to navigate it through the layered stages of prediction, activity, and consequence. The semiotic markers of the lavascape engender shifts in comprehension of those seeing, hearing, and experiencing both the durability and limitations of law performing as the manager of the unstable.

Yet, the performativity of law creates an illusion of stability in an environment of interpretive hazards. Can we really control calamity? Or, should we just tease the lava or the geyser knowing we have very little control. Law's authority over the dynamic relationship of the sightseer to the spectacle is tempered and revealed as illusory when ropes are crossed but no one gets hurt. The negotiation of common sense positions the individual against law in the self-determination of risk in naturally kinetic terrains. Law ironically hopes we will use our own best judgment. Paradoxically, movement and materiality in kinetic terrains challenge law's normative governing capacity in fleeting moments whether in public parks, on private land, or standing near a stream of oozing molten lava or boiling bubbles.

Bibliography

Appadurai, Arjun and Carol A. Breckenridge. 2009. "Forward." In *Soak: Mumbai in an Estuary*, edited by Anuradha Mathur and Dilip da Cunha, viii–ix. New Delhi: Rupa.

Associated Press. 2014. "Hawaii Brothers Sell Concert-Like Lava Tee Shirts." *Hawaii News Now*, December 12, 2014. https://www.hawaiinewsnow.com/story/27616303/hawaii-brothers-sell-concert-like-lava-tee-shirts/

Associated Press and Alexandra Klausner. 2014. "'I Felt Like My Face was Burning': Hawaii Couple Arrested for Trespassing to Get Close to Molten Lava to Take Selfies and Dip Household Items." https://www.dailymail.co.uk/news/article-2816859/I-felt-like-face-burning-Hawaii-couple-arrested-trespassing-close-molten-lava-SELFIES-dip-household-items.html

Bain, Carolyn and Alexis Averbuck. 2015. *Lonely Planet: Iceland.* Lonely Planet Publications.

Barr, Olivia. 2016. *A Jurisprudence of Movement: Common Law, Walking, Unsettling Place.* New York: Routledge.

Bartel, Robyn, Nicole Graham, Sue Jackson, Jason Hugh Prior, Daniel Francis Robinson, Meg Sherval, and Stewart Williams. 2013. "Legal Geography: An Australian Perspective." *Geographical Research* 51(4): 339–353.

Benda-Beckmann, Franz and Keebet Benda-Beckmann. 2014. "Places That Come and Go: A Legal Anthropological Perspective on the Temporalities of Space in Plural Legal Orders." In *The Expanding Spaces of Law: A Timely Legal Geography*, edited by Irus Braverman, Nicholas Blomley, David Delaney, and Alexandre Kedar, 30–52. Stanford, CA: Stanford University Press.

Bennett, Jane. 2010. *Vibrant Matter: A Political Ecology of Things*. Durham: Duke University Press.

Big Island Now. 2014. "Agreement Reached for Two Land Chain of Craters Road." Big Island Now, October 21, 2014. https://bigislandnow.com/2014/10/21/agreement-reached-for-two-lane-chain-of-craters-road/

Big Island Video News. 2014. "VIDEO: Claimor for Lava Diversion Booed at Pahoa Meeting." Big Island Video News, September 3, 2014. http://www.bigislandvideonews.com/2014/09/03/video-clamor-lava-diversion-booed-pahoa-meeting/

Big Island Video News. 2018(a). "DLNR Responds to Criticism Over Sea Turtles Killed by Lava." *Big Island Video News*. July 24, 2018. http://www.bigislandvideonews.com/2018/07/24/dlnr-responds-to-criticism-over-lava-response/

Big Island Video News. 2018(b). "Hawaii Eruption: Lava Viewing Area Plans Revealed." *Big Island Video News*. October 4, 2018. http://www.bigislandvideonews.com/2018/10/04/video-lava-viewing-area-plans-revealed/

Blomley, Nicholas. 2011. *Rights of Passage: Sidewalks and the Regulation of Public Flow*. New York: Routledge.

Blomley, Nicholas, David Delaney, and Richard T. Ford. 2001. *The Legal Geographies Reader*. Malden, MA: Blackwell.

Boyette, Chris. 2018. "Hawaii Officials Didn't Know Coast Guard Let Tour Boats Get Closer to Lava." *CNN*, July 19, 2018. https://www.cnn.com/2018/07/19/us/hawaii-lava-bomb-boat-coast-guard/index.html

Braverman, Irus. 2012. *Zooland: The Institution of Captivity*. Stanford, CA: Stanford University Press.

Braverman, Irus. 2013. *Zooland: The Institution of Captivity*. Stanford: Stanford University Press.

Braverman, Irus, Nicholas Blomley, David Delaney, and Alexandre Kedar. 2014. *The Expanding Spaces of Law: A Timely Legal Geography*. Stanford: Stanford University Press.

Brigham, John. 1990. *Property and the Politics of Entitlement*. Philadelphia: Temple University Press.

Brigham, John. 2009a. "Seeing Jurisdiction: Some Jurisprudential Issues Arising from Law Being '…All Over'." *Law & Policy* 31(4): 381–404.

Brigham, John. 2009b. *Material Law: A Jurisprudence of What's Real*. Philadelphia: Temple University Press.

Chiu, Allyson. 2018. "Hawai'i's Volcanoes: How George S. Patton Took on the Lava with Bombs." *Washington Post,* May 17, 2018. Accessed 17 December 2018. https://www.washingtonpost.com/news/morning-mix/wp/2018/05/17/hawaiis-volcanoes-how-george-s-patton-took-on-the-lava-and-lost/?noredirect=on&utm_term=.095e6f597ab3

William, Cole and Nakaso Dan. 2018. "2014 Lava Flow Spared Pahoa of Devastation" *Star Advertiser*, May 4, 2018. https://www.staradvertiser.com/2018/05/04/hawaii-news/2014-lava-flow-spared-pahoa-of-devastation/

Coombes, Brad, Jay T. Johnson, and Richard Howitt. 2012. "Indigenous Geographies II: The Aspirational Spaces in Postcolonial Politics – Reconciliation, Belonging, and Social Provision." *Progress in Human Geography* 37(5): 691–700.

Cooper, George and Gavan Daws. 1985. *Land and Power in Hawaii: The Democratic Years*. Honolulu: University of Hawai'i Press.

Cunningham, Kevin. 2018. "PHOTO: Golfers Brave Erupting Volcano in Hawaii to Sneak in a Round" *Golf*, May 16, 2018. https://golf.com/travel/photos-golfers-brave-erupting-volcano-in-hawaii-to-sneak-in-a-round/

Davies, Margaret. 2017. *Law Unlimited: Materialism, Pluralism, and Legal Theory*. New York: Routledge.

De León, Jason. 2015. *The Land of Open Graves: Living and Dying on the Migrant Trail*. Oakland: University of California Press.

Delaney, David. 2010. *Nomospheric Investigations: The Spatial, the Legal, and the Pragmatics of World-Making*. New York: Routledge.

Department of Land and Natural Resources (State of Hawai'i), Amendment and Compilation of Chapter 13–222 Hawaii Administrative Rules, Adopted December 13, 2002. https://dlnr.hawaii.gov/ld/files/2013/07/Ch13-222-Amend-Compil-Stand-Rev1.pdf

Donnelly, Christine. 2018. "Big Island Lava-Land Owners Get a Tax Break, Not a Buyout." *Star Advertiser*, May 18, 2018. https://www.staradvertiser.com/2018/05/18/hawaii-news/kokua-line/big-island-lava-land-owners-get-a-tax-break-not-a-buyout/

Dorsett, Shaunnagh and Shaun McVeigh. 2012. *Jurisdiction*. New York: Routledge.

Dovey, Kim. 1999. *Framing Places: Mediating Power in Built Form*. New York: Routledge.

Dudziak, Mary L. and Leti Volpp. 2006. *Legal Borderlands: Law and the Construction of American Borders*. Baltimore: John Hopkins University Press.

Einarsson, Þorleifur. 1974. *The Heimaey Eruption in Words and Pictures*. Trans. Alan Boucher. Reykjavik: Heimskringla.

Ewick, Patricia and Susan S. Silbey. 1998. *The Common Place of Law: Stories from Everyday Life*. Chicago: University of Chicago Press.

Ford, Alexander Hume. 1911. Editorial Comment, *The Mid-Pacific Magazine* (March 1911), Vol. 1, No. 3, Territory of Hawai'i.

Ford, Richard T. 2001. "Law's Territory (A History of Jurisdiction)." In *The Legal Geographies Reader*, edited by Nicholas Blomley, David Delaney, and Richard T. Ford, 200–217. Malden, MA: Blackwell.

Foucault, Michel. 1991. "Governmentality." In *The Foucault Effect: Studies in Governmentality*, edited by Graham Burchell, Colin Gordon, and Peter Miller, 87–104. Chicago: University of Chicago Press.

Frear, Walter F. 1911. Opening to *The Mid-Pacific Magazine, Vol. 1, No. 3* published monthly by Alexander Hume Ford, Honolulu; copyright 1911.

Fujimori, Leila. 2018. "Leilani Estates Returnees Assess Lava Damage." *Star Advertiser*, Sept. 11, 2018. http://www.staradvertiser.com/2018/09/11/hawaii-news/leilani-estates-returnees-assess-lava-damage/

Goodyear-Ka'ōpua, Ikaika Hussey, and Erin Kahunawaika'ala Wright. 2014. *A Nation Rising: Hawaiian Movements for Life, Land, and Sovereignty*. Durham: Duke University Press.

Hacking, Ian. 2003. "Risk and Dirt." In *Risk and Morality*, edited by Richard V. Ericson and Aaron Doyle, 22–47. Toronto: University of Toronto Press.

Hajek, Danny. 2014. "Diverting Lava Flow May Be Possible, But Some Hawaiians Object." *National Public Radio*, November 1, 2014. https://www.npr.org/2014/11/01/360719232/diverting-lava-flow-may-be-possible-but-some-hawaiians-object

Hale, Benjamin. 2016. *The Wild and the Wicked: On Nature and Human Nature*. Cambridge, MA: MIT Press.

Harvey, David. 1996. *Justice, Nature and the Geography of Difference*. Malden, MA: Blackwell.

Hawaii Center for Volcanology, Hosted at School of Ocean and Earth Science and Technology, University of Hawaii at Manoa. https://www.soest.hawaii.edu/GG/HCV/kil-hist.html

Hawai'i County Civil Defense. http://www.hawaiicounty.gov/civil-defense/

Hawai'i Emergency Management Agency, State of Hawai'i. 2017. "Recent Collapses at the Kamokuna Ocean Entry Underscore On-Going Hazard" March 8, 2017. http://dod.hawaii.gov/hiema/kilaueas-on-going-hazard/

Hawaii News Now. 2012. "Lava Claims Final Home in Royal Gardens Subdivision". March 3, 2012. http://www.hawaiinewsnow.com/story/17073848/lava-claims-final-home-in-royal-gardens-subdivision

Hawaii News Now. 2018. "State Eyes 'Lava Bridge,' Other Fixes to Keep Key Roadways Open." Hawaii News Now, May 14, 2018. https://www.hawaiinewsnow.com/story/38189192/state-eyes-lava-bridge-other-fixes-to-keep-key-roadways-open/

Hawai'i Volcanoes National Park. n.d (a) "Hawaii Volcanoes National Park Creates $166 Million in Economic Benefits." Accessed 17 December 2018. https://www.nps.gov/havo/learn/news/20180426_pr_visitation.htm

Hawai'i Volcanoes National Park. n.d (b). "What's Going on With the Volcano?" Accessed 18 December 2018. https://www.nps.gov/havo/planyourvisit/lava2.htm

Hawaiian Volcano Observatory. n.d. "Frequently Asked Questions and Answers about Lava-Flow Hazards." *Volcano Hazards Program*. https://volcanoes.usgs.gov/observatories/hvo/faq_lava.html

Hawaiian Volcano Observatory. n.d. (2). "Lava Flow Hazards Zones and Flow Forecast Methods, Island of Hawai'i." *Volcano Hazards Program*. https://volcanoes.usgs.gov/observatories/hvo/hawaii_lava_flows.html

Hawaiian Volcano Observatory. n.d. "The Pu'u 'Ō'ō Eruption Lasted 35 Years." https://volcanoes.usgs.gov/volcanoes/kilauea/geo_hist_1983.html

Hawaiian Volcano Observatory. n.d. "Volcano Watch: Who Owns New Coastal Lands Created by Lava Flows?" May 1, 2008. Accessed 28 April 2020. https://volcanoes.usgs.gov/observatories/hvo/hvo_volcano_watch.html?vwid=432

Hawaiian Volcano Observatory. 2017. "Did Aerial Bombing Stop the 1935 Mauna Loa Lava Flow?" *West Hawaii Today* December 1, 2017. https://www.westhawaiitoday.com/2017/12/01/hawaii-news/volcano-update/did-aerial-bombing-stop-the-1935-mauna-loa-lava-flow/

Helsel, Phil and Erin Calabrese. 2018. "Once the Lava Stops, Rebuilding and Futures Uncertain in Hawaii" *NBC News*, May 12, 2018. https://www.nbcnews.com/news/weather/once-lava-stops-rebuilding-futures-uncertain-hawaii-n873581

Iceland, Monitor. 2016. "Geysir Food Dye Artist Found Not Guilty." *Iceland Monitor*, July 6, 2016. https://icelandmonitor.mbl.is/news/nature_and_travel/2016/07/06/geysir_food_dye_artist_found_not_guilty/

Immerwahr, Daniel. 2019. *How to Hide an Empire: A History of the Greater United States*. New York: Farrar, Straus, and Giroux.

Ingold, Tim. 2007. *Lines: A Brief History*. New York: Routledge.

Jacobs, Julia. 2018. "Lava Bomb Hits Tourist Boat in Hawaii, Injuring 23." *New York Times*, July 17, 2018. https://www.nytimes.com/2018/07/17/us/lava-bomb-boat-video-hawaii.html

Jaggar, Thomas A. 1916. *Honolulu Star Bulletin*, Aug. 15, 1916. http://chroniclingamerica.loc.gov/lccn/sn82014682/1916-08-15/ed-2/seq-9.pdf

Johnson, Kristen. 2017. "Bicycle, Food Venders Cashing in at Gateway to Kamokuna Lava Flow." *Hawaii Tribune Herald*, August 13, 2017. https://www.hawaiitribune-herald.com/2017/08/13/hawaii-news/bicycle-food-vendors-cashing-in-at-gateway-to-kamokuna-lava-flow/

Jones, Reece. 2012. *Border Walls: Security and the War on Terror in the United States*. India, and Israel. London: Zed Books.

Jones, Reece. 2016. *Violent Borders: Refugees and the Right to Move*. New York: Verso.

Jonsson, Patrik. 2014. "Lava Inches Toward Hawaii Community: Kilauea's Tutu Pele Spirit Strikes Again?" *The Christian Science Monitor*, September 6, 2014. https://www.csmonitor.com/USA/2014/0906/Lava-inches-toward-Hawaii-community-Kilauea-s-Tutu-Pele-spirit-strikes-again

Katz, Brigit. 2020. "Found: Two Bombs from 1935 Stuck in Hawai'i Volcano." *Smithsonian* March 17, 2020. https://www.smithsonianmag.com/smart-news/found-two-bombs-dropped-hawaii-volcano-1935-180974429/

Kedar, Alexandre. 2014. "Expanding Legal Geographies: A Call for a Critical Comparative Approach." In *The Expanding Spaces of Law: A Timely Legal Geography*, edited by Irus Braverman, Nicholas Blomley, David Delaney, and Alexandre Kedar, 95–119. Stanford, CA: Stanford University Press.

Klinke, Ian. 2012. "Chronopolitics: A Conceptual Matrix." *Process in Human Geography* 37(5): 673–690.

Kobayashi, v. Zimring [566 P.2d 725 (1977)]

Kohn, Margaret. 2004. *Brave New Neighborhoods: The Privatization of Public Space*. New York: Routledge.

Ganga, La and L. Maria 2014. "Lava's Slow Approach is Reshaping Life." *Los Angeles Times*, November 3, 2014. https://www.westhawaiitoday.com/2014/11/03/hawaii-news/lavas-slow-approach-is-reshaping-life/

Lauer, Nancy Cook. 2018. "Mayor Says Restricting Construction in Lava Zones 1 and 2 Would Be Counterproductive." *West Hawaii Today*, July 11, 2018. https://www.hawaiitribune-herald.com/2018/07/11/hawaii-news/mayor-says-restricting-construction-in-lava-zones-1-and-2-would-be-counterproductive/

Law, John. 2004. *After Method: Mess in Social Science Research*. New York: Routledge.

Law, John and Vicky Singleton. 2005. "Object Lessons." *Organization* 12(3): 331–355.

Levinson, Sanford. 1998. *Constitutional Faith*. Princeton, NJ: Princeton University Press.

Lincoln, Mileka. 2014. "Pahoa Property Owner's Berm Raises Legal Concerns, Worries Neighbors." *Hawaii News Now*, October 29, 2014. https://www.hawaiinewsnow.com/story/27159878/phoa-property-owners-berm-raises-legal-concerns-worries-neighbors/

Linklater, Andro. 2013. *Owning the Earth: The Transforming History of Land Ownership*. New York: Bloomsbury.

Lockwood, J.P. and F.A. Torgerson. 1980. "Diversion of Lava Flows by Aerial Bombing – Lessons from Mauna Loa Volcano, Hawaii." *Bulletin Volcanologique* 43: 727–741.

MacCannell, Dean. 2013. *The Tourist: A New Theory of the Leisure Class*. Berkeley: University of California Press.

MacDonald, Gordon A. 1962. "The 1959 and 1960 Eruptions of Kilauea Volcano, Hawaii, and the Construction of Walls to Restrict the Spread of the Lava Flows." *Bulletin Volcanologique* 24: 249–294.

Maly, Kepā and Maly Onaona. 2005. *He Wahi Mo'olelo No Keauhou A Me Na Wahi Pana Ma Laila: A Collection of Traditions, Historical Accounts and Kama'āina Recollections of Keauhou and its Stories Places: With Notes from Adjoining Lands in Ka'ū and Puna, Island of Hawai'i*. Kumu Pono Associates, LLC, Hilo, Hawai'i.

Marusek, Sarah. 2012. "Lawnscape: Semiotics of Space, Spectacle, and Ownership,"*Social Semiotics* 22(4): 447–458.

Marusek, Sarah. 2014. "Emblem of Folk Legality: Semiotic Prosecution and the American Bald Eagle." In *Law, Culture, and Visual Studies*, edited by Richard K. Sherwin and Anne Wagner, 497–512. London: Springer.

Marusek, Sarah. 2016. *Politics of Parking: Rights, Identity, and Property*. New York: Routledge.

Marusek, Sarah. 2017. "Exploring Layers of Law and the Sensory at the Volcano." In *Synesthetic Legalities: Sensory Dimensions of Law and Jurisprudence*, edited by Sarah Marusek, 1–8. New York: Routledge.

Marusek, Sarah. 2019. "Lavascape: Legal Spectacle at Kīlauea." *Social Semiotics* 29(3): 351–363.

Marusek, Sarah. 2020. "Parking Policy: The Socio-Legal Architecture of Parking Bays in American Cities." *Land Use Policy*, 91(103931) https://doi.org/10.1016/j.landusepol.2019.03.044

Marusek, Sarah and John Brigham. 2017. *Street Level Sovereignty: The Intersection of Space and Law*. Lanham, MD: Lexington Books.

Matsunami, Osamu W. 1974. "Subdivision Development in Lower Puna, Hawaii." Thesis, Department of Geography, University of Hawaii, Hilo College, Dec. 23, 1974.

Meyer, Manulani Aluli. 2003. *Ho'oulu: Our Time of Becoming: Collected Early Writings of Manulani Meyer*. Honolulu: 'Ai Pōhaku Press.

Minow, Martha, Michael Ryan, and Austin Sarat. 1995. *Narrative, Violence, and the Law: The Essays of Robert Cover (Law, Meaning and Violence)*. Ann Arbor: University of Michigan Press.

Moniz Nakamura, Jadelyn. 2003. *Keonehelelei: Archeological Inventory Survey of the Footprints National Register Site Ahupua'a of Kapapala, Hawai'I Volcanoes National Park*. National Park Service, U.S. Department of the Interior. https://www.nps.gov/havo/learn/historyculture/upload/20060908_Keonehelelei_508.pdf

Moniz Nakamura, Jadelyn. 2010. *Gathering on the Rim: People Build a Park*. Hawai'i Volcanoes National Park Occasional Papers, Volume 1, Number 2, Fall 2010. National Park Service, U.S. Department of the Interior, 1–49.

Nishida, Jean I. 1975. "Subdivision Land Onwership Patterns in Puna, Hawaii." Thesis, Department of Geography, University of Hawaii, Hilo College, August 14, 1975.

O'Malley, Pat. 2004. "The Government of Risks." In *The Blackwell Companion to Law and Society*, edited by Austin Sarat, 292–308. Malden, MA: Blackwell.

Paiva, Derek. 2008. "'Lava House' Resident on Anthony Bourdain Show OK." *Hawai'i Magazine*, March 5, 2008. https://www.hawaiimagazine.com/blogs/hawaii_today/2008/3/5/Lava_House_resident_Anthony_Bourdain_OK

Philippopoulos-Mihalopoulos, Andreas. 2013. "Atmospheres of Law: Senses, Affects, Lawscapes." *Emotion, Space, and Society* 7: 35–44.

Philippopoulos-Mihalopoulos, Andreas. 2015. *Spatial Justice: Body, Lawscape, Atmosphere*. New York: Routledge.

Philippopoulos-Mihalopoulos, Andreas. 2018. "And For Law: Why Space Cannot Be Understood Without Law." *Law, Culture, and the Humanities.* DOI: 10.1177/1743872118765708.

Platt, Rutherford H. 2004. *Land Use and Society: Geography, Law, and Public Policy*. London: Island Press.

Purdy, Jedidiah. 2010. *The Meaning of Property: Freedom, Community, and the Legal Imagination*. New Haven: Yale University Press.

Richland, Justin B. 2007. "Pragmatic Paradoxes and Ironies of Indigeneity at the 'Edge' of Hope Sovereignty." *American Ethnologist* 34(3): 540–557.

Rubin, Ken. n.d. "Historical Eruptions of Kilauea Volcano." *Hawaii Center for Volcanology*. Accessed 17 December 2018. http://www.soest.hawaii.edu/GG/HCV/kil-hist.html

Salmons, Stephanie. 2019. “Despite Delays Caused by Hot Lava Rock, Highway 132 Could Reopen Next Month.” *Hawaii Tribune Herald*, October 4, 2019. https://www.hawaiitribune-herald.com/2019/10/04/hawaii-news/despite-delays-caused-by-hot-lava-rock-highway-132-could-reopen-next-month/

Sarat, Austin. 1990. “The Law Is All Over’: Power, Resistance, and the Legal Consciousness of the Welfare Poor.” *Yale Journal of Law & the Humanities* 2(2): 343–379.

Scott, James C. 1998. *Seeing Like a State: How Certain Schemes to Improve the Human Condition Have Failed*. New Haven: Yale University Press.

Seo, Sarah A. 2019. *Policing the Open Road: How Cars Transformed American Freedom*. Cambridge, MA: Harvard University Press.

Serafin, Peter. 2014. “On Hawaii Island, Watching a Disaster Flow Ever Closer.” *Los Angeles Times*, September 27, 2014. https://www.latimes.com/nation/la-na-hawaii-lava-20140928-story.html

Sganga, Caterina. 2018. *Propertizing European Copyright: History, Challenges and Opportunities*. Cheltenham: Edward Elgar.

Simon, Jonathan. 2007. *Governing through Crime: How the War on Crime Transformed American Democracy and Created a Culture of Fear*. New York: Oxford University Press.

Spence, Mark David. 1999. *Dispossessing the Wilderness: Indian Removal and the Making of the National Parks*. New York: Oxford University Press.

Stack, Liam. 2019. “A Tourist Wanted a Better Look at an Active Volcano. Then He Fell In.” *New York Times*, May 2, 2019. https://www.nytimes.com/2019/05/02/us/man-falls-hawaii-volcano.html

State of Hawai’i. 2018. Hazard Mitigation Plan. Section 4 Risk Assessment. https://dod.hawaii.gov/hiema/files/2018/06/Draft-Section-4.15-Wildfire-Placeholder.pdf

Steinberg, Theodore. 1995. *Slide Mountain: Or the Folly of Owning Nature*. Berkeley: University of California Press.

Stone, Christopher. 2010. *Should Trees Have Standing? Law Morality and the Environment*. New York: Oxford University Press.

Thurston, Lorrin A. 1911. *The Mid-Pacific Magazine*, Vol. 1, No. 3, March 1911, p. 303.

Turner, Nicholas R., Ryan L. Perroy, and Ken Hon. 2017. “Lava Flow Hazard Prediction and Monitoring with UAS: A Case Study from the 2014–2015 Pāhoa Lava Flow Crisis, *Hawai’i*.” *Journal of Applied Volcanology* 6 (17). DOI: 10.1186/s13617-017-0068-3.

Tyler, Tom (1990). *Why People Obey the Law*. Princeton: Princeton University Press.

Tyler, Tom. 2006. *Why People Obey the Law*. Princeton, NJ: Princeton University Press.

U.S. Department of the Interior and U.S. Geological Survey n.d. “U.S. Geological Survey Programs in Hawaii and the Pacific.” Accessed 28 April 2020. https://pubs.usgs.gov/fs/FS-011-96/fs-011-96.pdf

United States Geological Survey, n.d. Volcano Hazards Program “Pu‘u ‘Ō’ō and the Current Eruption of Kīlauea.” https://volcanoes.usgs.gov/volcanoes/kilauea/geo_hist_1983.html

United States Geological Survey. 2019. “Volcano Hazards Program: Maps.” December 18, 2019. https://volcanoes.usgs.gov/volcanoes/kilauea/multimedia_maps.html

Valverde, Mariana. 2003. *Law’s Dream of a Common Knowledge*. Princeton: Princeton University Press.

Valverde, Mariana. 2012. *Everyday Law on the Street: City Governance in an Age of Diversity*. Chicago: University of Chicago Press.

Valverde, Mariana. 2014. "'Time Thickens, Takes on Flesh': Spatiotemporal Dynamics in Law." In *The Expanding Spaces of Law: A Timely Legal Geography*, edited by Irus Braverman, Nicholas Blomley, David Delaney, and Alexandre (Sandy) Kedar, 53–76. Stanford: Stanford University Press.

Wagner, Anne. 2006. "The Rules of the Road, a Universal Visual Semiotics." *International Journal for the Semiotics of Law* 19(3): 311–324.

Weiner, Mark. 2006. *Americans without Law: The Racial Boundaries of Citizenship*. New York: NYU Press.

Whittlesey, Lee H. 2014. *Death in Yellowstone: Accidents and Foolhardiness in the First National Park*. Rinehart: Roberts Publishers.

Wright, Thomas L., Jon Y.F. Chun, Jean Exposo, Christina Heliker, Jon Hodge, John P. Lockwood, and Susan M. Vogt. 1992. "Map Showing Lava-Flow Hazard Zones, Island of Hawaii" U.S. Geological Survey Miscellaneous Field Studies Map MF-2193. https://pubs.usgs.gov/mf/1992/2193/

Wu, Nina. 2018. "6 More Citations Issued to Lava Loiters in Lower Puna." *Star Advertiser*, June 19, 2018. Accessed 17 December 2018. http://www.staradvertiser.com/2018/06/19/breaking-news/six-more-citations-issued-to-lava-loiterers-in-lower-puna/

Yanow, Dvora and Peregrine Schwartz-Shea. 2006. *Interpretation and Method: Empirical Research Methods and the Interpretive Turn*. Armonk, NY: M.E. Sharpe.

Index

Italicized pages refer to figures.

accreted land 30–31, 33, 34, 93
American-based common sense 79
Association of Zoos and Aquariums (AZA) 22

Bakhtin, M.M. 65
Bartel, Robyn 7
Blue Lagoon 4, 5
Bourdain, Anthony 30
Braverman, Irus 22
Brigham, John 8, 89

Chain of Craters Road 72–73
chaos 7
chronotopes 65
cinder 30
Civil Defense 67, 78
common sense: American-based 79; engendering 72; generalized 77; individual 88, 90; negotiations of 84–90; semiotics of 75
Cover, Robert 13
Crawford, Ruth 84
culture: dynamism of 33; entrepreneurial 15; and law 13; as a manager of risk 77

Davies, Margaret 8
Delaney, David 68
disasters: in the making 70; ongoing 70; public quality of 51–55; sudden 70; unpredictable 70; *see also* natural phenomena
Dorsett, Shaunnagh 69
dynamic landscape: Hawai'i 3–9; Iceland 4–9; law within 10; overview 6

East Rift Zone 68
ebbs and flows of terrain 58–61
epistemologies: of jurisdiction 19–35; kinetic, of nature as property 30–33; native, about Kîlauea 26
eruption: heterotemporality of 62–69; regulating 80–81
Evaristti, Marco 84
Ewick, Patricia 44
Executive Order No. 83 27

Federal Aviation Administration (FAA) 53
Federal Emergency Management Agency 39
First Amendment 24
fissure map *69*
fluid landscape 2
"folk geographies" 48–49
"folk legalities" 48–49
Ford, Alexander Hume 21–22, 23
Foucault, Michel 76
Frear, Walter F. 26

geothermal energy 5
geothermal spas 4–5
GIS 67
Government Road System 21

Hacking, Ian 88
Halema'uma'u Crater 15, 43–45, 48, 52, 57–58, 62, 74, 85
hâpu'u (tree fern) 20
Hawai'i: dynamic landscape 3–4; and lava 9; scientific and cultural directives 10–11; volcanic environment in 1
Hawaiian archipelago 72

Hawaiian Volcano Observatory (HVO) 22, 26, 42, 49, 60–62; earthquake map *64*
Hawai'i Center for Volcanology 28
Hawai'i County Civil Defense 78
Hawai'i County Civil Defense Agency 15, 39–40, 47, 67
Hawai'i Island 37–38, 49
Hawai'i State Department of Land and Natural Resources 54
Hawaii Tribune Herald 50
Hawaii Tribune-Herald 80
Hawai'i Volcanoes National Park (HVNP) 3, 19–20, 22–24, 27, 29, 37, 60, 68–69, 75; Chain of Craters Road 72–73; sign at Devastation Hiking Trail on crater's rim within *87*; trail in 88
Hawaii Volcano Research Association 22
hazard: containing the lava 80–81; legal semiotics of 75–81; regulating eruption 80–81
heterotemporality of eruption 62–69

Iceland: dynamic landscape 4–9; geothermal spas 4–5; scientific and cultural directives 10–11; volcanic environment in 1
"interstitial zones of hybridization" 59

Jaggar, Thomas A. 22, 26
Jaggar Museum 22, 45, 52, 54
Jehovah Witnesses 24
Johnson, Kristen 50
jurisdiction: epistemologies of 19–35; of land 21; *see also* law

Kamâmalu, Victoria 20
Kamehameha I, founder of the Kingdom of Hawai'i 20
Kapeau, George L. 21
kapu (traditional laws and customs) 20
Kedar, Sandy 47
Kenoi, Billy 73
Keonehelelei 32
Keoni Ana 21
Kîlauea 1–2, 3, *4*, 19–20, 57, 59–60; American quest for ownership of 20, 24–26; and East Rift Zone *66*, 68; Hawaiians denied ownership of 27; lava eruption from 38; and law 7; Madame Pele, the Hawaiian Goddess of Fire 19–22; National Park Service 24; native epistemologies about 26; overview 19; ownership as a National Park by U.S. government 29; and *terra incognita* 24–25; volcanic eruption *42*
Kîlauea Caldera 79
Kîlauea Iki 75; volcano eruption *76*
Kim, Harry 68, 81
kineticism 11; of law 2; and legal performativity 37–51; and natural environment 13
kinetic landscape 17
King Kamehameha III 21
"knowing the ropes": legal semiotics of hazard 75–81; negotiations of common sense 84–90; teasing the spectacle 81–84
Kobayashi v. Zimring 30
Kohala Volcano 60
kuleana (responsibility, well-being) 20

land, layering of 69–74
landscape mapping 16
lava 37; containing 80–81; covering pavement within Hawai'i Volcanoes National Park *73*; eruption from Kîlauea 38; flow thickness map *65*; flow travel times based on actual flow rates *63*; glow 38–39; and legal responses 8–9; mappings of 16; as metaphor for law 2; *see also* molten lava
Lava Entry Safety Zone 53
Lava Loiters 54
lavascape 9–18; accretion of law in 33–35; as volcanic spectacle 38
lava-viewing areas *49*, 50
Lava Zone Map 48, 59, 61, 67, 72
Lava Zone One 16, 31
law: and boundaries 46; and culture 13; in daily life 1; defined 44; within dynamic environments 10; and Kîlauea 7; kineticism of 2; and landscape change 10; lava as metaphor for 2; management of the unstable 22–27; regulating natural spectacle 18; as spectacle 6; and Western social order 2
lawscape 8–9; of Philippopoulos-Mihalopoulos 38
layering of land and legality 69–74
legal geography 9, 11
legality: layering of land and 69–74; modern 92

legal landscape 8, 33
legal performativity: and kineticism 37–51
legal perspectivism 15
legal positivism 28
legal semiotics of hazard 75–81
Leilani eruption 52–53, 55
Leilani Estates 3, 16, 29, 31, 34, 38, 40, 51, 55

Madame Pele, the Hawaiian Goddess of Fire 3, 8, 17, 19–22, 38, 43–44
Magno, Talmadge 50
mapping, landscape 16
Mauna Loa 62, 80, 82
McVeigh, Shaun 69
Metcalf, Brady 80
Metcalf, Myke 80
The Mid-Pacific Magazine 21
Miura, Lisa 30
molten lava 37; glow 38–40; as spectacle 38; *see also* lava

National Guard 78, 80; Humvee 78
National Park rangers 78
natural phenomena: and private lands 47; and public lands 47; *see also* disasters
No Reservations (Bourdain) 30

Okabe, Wil 54
ongoing disasters 70
Orlando, Cindy 73
ownership 29; Kîlauea, as National Park by U.S. government 29; of land 2; *see also* property

Pâhoa 38
Patton, George S. 8
Pele, Tutu 71, 74, 80, 82, 89
Philippopoulos-Mihalopoulos, Andreas 8
property: kinetic epistemologies of nature as 30–33; *see also* ownership of land
Pu'u 'Ō'ō volcanic cone 3

Queen Lili'uokalani of the Kingdom of Hawai'i 47

regulating eruption 80–81
responsibility, defined 38
Richardson, C. E. 20
Rift Zones 60
risk 76–77; and culture 77; in kinetic environments 77; knowledge of 77
risk of natural events: and law 14; *see also* disasters

Sarat, Austin 15
Schatz, Brian 73
Schwartz-Shea, Peregrine 13
Scott, James C. 44, 61
Sganga, Caterina 28
Silbey, Susan S. 44
spectacle(s): lavascape as volcanic 38; law as 6; molten lava as 38; public quality of 51–55; regulations associated with 47; volcano as 6
Steinberg, Theodore 31–32, 89
Strokkur Geyser 4, *5*, 57, 62, 74, *85*; warnings at *87*
sudden disasters 70
Swain, F.B. 20

terrain: ebbs and flows of 58–61; mapping projects of 58–59
terra incognita 21, 24, 32, 34
Thingvellir National Park 4
Thompson, Jack 30, 62
Thurston, Lorrin A. 22, 23, 24–26, 32
Thurston Lava Tube 23
topologies of governance: ebbs and flows of terrain 58–61; heterotemporality of eruption 62–69; layering of land and legality 69–74; overview 57–58
tourism 37

United States Geological Survey (USGS) 16, 28, 31, 48, 59, 61, 67; Hawai'i Island lava hazard map *60*; and hazard information 72; Lava Zone Map 59
unpredictable disasters 70
U.S. Air Force 80
U.S. Department of the Interior 27, 39, 88

Valverde, Mariana 65
volcano: Kîlauea Volcano 1–2, 3, *4*, 19–20; as spectacle 6; *see also* lava
von Benda-Beckmann, Franz 48
von Benda-Beckmann, Keebet 48

Wilson, Woodrow 3

Yanow, Dvora 13
Yellowstone National Park 57

For Product Safety Concerns and Information please contact our EU representative GPSR@taylorandfrancis.com
Taylor & Francis Verlag GmbH, Kaufingerstraße 24, 80331 München, Germany

www.ingramcontent.com/pod-product-compliance
Ingram Content Group UK Ltd.
Pitfield, Milton Keynes, MK11 3LW, UK
UKHW011020180926
475701UK00004B/846

9780367698126